Praise for *Mothering with Courage*

"It is one thing to read a book about parenting. It is another to have a resource which provides the tools to help us create authentic, influential relationships with our children. *Mothering with Courage* offers moms an easy-to-follow roadmap of self-discovery exercises designed to unlock their inner awareness and guide them to release the expectations and fears that prevent them from deeply connecting with their children in meaningful ways. It may be for mothers, but all parents can learn from this kind of self-exploration—and all of our children will benefit."

—Lori Petro, TEACH through Love founder
and speaker, parent educator, and child advocate

"A child's relationship with their mother is sacred. It is through her courage and intention that a mother learns to rise above the challenges of parenthood, become self-confident while seeing the beauty in her child. *Mothering with Courage* is the perfect gift for all mothers and children!"

—Dave Pelzer, author of *A Child Called It*
and *Too Close to Me*

"What an eloquent, compassionate guide to parenting from the inside out—beautiful! Fostering self-awareness and mindfulness are two of the most important keys to conscious parenting. I love *Mothering with Courage*—it's the perfect book to keep at your bedside and to continue to anchor back to as a reminder of how to stay connected to your children and to your soul. I can't wait to gift this to my family members and clients. Highly recommended for all parents!"

—Renee Peterson Trudeau, coach/speaker and author of *The Mother's Guide to Self-Renewal* and *Nurturing the Soul of Your Family*

"*Mothering with Courage* offers a blueprint for parenting from a deep awareness. Bonnie offers ways of incorporating positive messages while acknowledging negative ones carried from previous generations. She provides tools to help heal emotional wounds and end fear-based mothering. A must-read for all mothers."

—Kathy Maher, Energy Healer and Family Constellation Therapist

"*Mothering with Courage* is rooted in emotional intelligence and deep caring for the overall relationship between mother and child. Bonnie Compton has written a wonderful book that you must add to your parenting library. Authentic, warm, and full of helpful advice, Compton's knowledge is what today's mothers need."

—Carrie Goldman, award-winning author of *Bullied: What Every Parent, Teacher, and Kid Needs to Know About Ending the Cycle of Fear*

"Oh wow! In a world where we often times feel we are on our own in parenting, *Mothering with Courage* is the guide book that I wish I'd had twenty-five years ago when my child was born.

It offers clear and compelling guidance to feel confident in parenting. It inspires all of us as moms to tap into our most precious resource of all: our sixth sense. And reminds us that we already have all of the answers . . . if we only listen. This is the essence of a Mother's intuition! It truly is a must-read!"

—Sarah Scott Putnam, Intuitive Life Coach,
"The Art of Intuitive Living" Program

Mothering
with
Courage

FAMILIUS

Published by Familius LLC, www.familius.com

Familius books are available at special discounts for bulk purchases, whether for sales promotions or for family or corporate use. For more information, contact Familius Sales at 559-876-2170 or email orders@familius.com.

Library of Congress Cataloging-in-Publication Data
2016962608

Print ISBN 9781944822637
Ebook ISBN 9781944822644
Hardcover ISBN 9781944822651

Printed in the United States of America

Edited by Lindsay Sandberg
Cover design by David Miles
Book design by Brooke Jorden

10 9 8 7 6 5 4 3 2 1

First Edition

Mothering
with
Courage

The Mindful Approach to
Becoming a Mom Who Listens More,
Worries Less, and Loves Deeply

BONNIE COMPTON
APRN, BC. CPNP

Dedicated to Greg, my champion, husband, life partner, and most loving supporter—our love only grows stronger.

And to our children—Erin, Sarah, Ashley, and Tyler—I love you. Thank you for teaching me to be a better mom and continuing to support and challenge me.

Also for Olive, Tessa, Charlie, and all the sweet grandchildren yet to come: you are my sunshine and my teachers.

Contents

Preface

Recently, I received a call from a frustrated mother who sounded overwhelmed and exhausted. She said, "I want to be a really good mother, but I feel totally lost. I've read so many parenting books, but their tips and techniques work for only a few days. I've not found any that have helped me be a better mother."

I have received many similar calls, so the degree of this mother's frustration did not surprise me. In my thirty years of counseling and coaching mothers, I've observed how overwhelmed they can become by their responsibilities of motherhood and how isolated and alone they can feel. Mothers share with me that, on many days, they are on automatic pilot, lost in survival mode. Many express regret for not being as good a parent as they want to be. Additionally, many mothers look back and lament, "I wish I had known better so I could have done better." It is for these lost and frustrated mothers that I wrote *Mothering with Courage*. It is for moms navigating the uncertain journey of motherhood. It is also for new mothers just beginning their journey.

The stories in this book are derived from my years of clinical experience. They are not representative of particular clients, but reflect experiences many mothers have shared. By providing you with guidance and knowledge early in mothering, I hope that you will be better equipped to consciously choose your own path and perhaps avoid much of the frustration and heartache I hear from mothers in my office.

It used to be that mothers relied on extended family and village elders for guidance in mothering. In our busy, often disconnected world, mothers now look to books or blogs by experts and moms "in the trenches" on how to raise their children. While many of those books and blogs focus on correcting a child's behavior or offering suggestions for a mother's self-care, *Mothering with Courage* provides guidance for mothers to self-reflect and dig deep to discover what is important to them from their own perspective. Only from that space can a mother discover how to be the best, most authentic mother for her child.

I'm convinced that as long as mothers look for answers outside themselves, they miss the opportunity to tap into their own inner knowing. Both in my professional work and my experience as a mother, I have witnessed the power of a mother's intuition. Inner knowing can be instrumental in guiding mothers as they make decisions for both themselves and their children. I've seen over and over again that mothers have the ability to be their own best parenting expert when they begin to know and trust their own wisdom.

Mothering with Courage is based on the process I've used with many mothers that I've worked with over the years. In fact, it is the process I recommended to the woman whose call I described above. A week later, she reported that this new approach gave her hope—hope that she was not alone, hope that things could get better, and hope that she could find a way to be a better mom. She said she felt she had come home to herself.

Mothering with Courage—How to Begin

This book is designed to help you ask the right questions, questions that will help you tap into your own intuition as a mom. *Mothering with Courage* is to be used as your own personal tool, so you can decide how you want to use it. You may choose to read it cover to cover, or you may choose to read a particular chapter that speaks to you. Each chapter is distinct and can be a complete lesson and journaling experience in itself. If your time is restricted, I suggest reading the summary at the beginning of each chapter and then spending the rest of your time working on the Journaling Exercises. I've also included Mindful Mothering Tips in the appendix that will help remind you when you get lost in the day-to-day activities and responsibilities. I invite you to utilize this book as the tool that you need, right now, to help you discover the mother you want to be!

I recommend scheduling time into your day to actually answer the questions. Create a special journal and keep it close at hand as you read the book and complete the journaling exercises. Your journal will become an invaluable guidebook for you in the future. It will serve as a conscious reminder of how you want to be as a mom. It's easy to let life distract you, but it takes time, courage, and a commitment to make positive changes in both yourself and your parenting. Most importantly, be gentle with yourself as you read and work through the book. Remind yourself that in the past, you did the best you could. Honor yourself for your courage and willingness to make positive changes in your life. Celebrate that your willingness to shift your own perspective and way of being will contribute to positive changes in your child and family. And, most importantly, celebrate the unique, awesome mom that you already are!

Remember: motherhood is a journey. I am honored by your interest and willingness to learn more about yourself and your children. And as you take this journey for you and your family, I hope you're able to self-reflect and find answers to some of your questions—or begin to ask new questions. Perhaps you will experience your own "wake up" moments. It is my hope and intention that as you embark on this journey, you will begin to find your own answers—that you will become self-reflective, make mindful decisions, and learn to trust your own intuition. As a result, you will begin to discover what really matters for you and your family.

Chapter 1

The Reflective Mom

Ask yourself if what you are doing today
is getting you closer to where
you want to be tomorrow.

—Unknown

*m*y family had an old station wagon with a back rear-facing seat. I thought riding in that seat, facing where I'd been, was a great adventure. At some point or another, you've experienced the adventure of riding backwards. It not only gives you the opportunity to explore what's behind you but is also a great metaphor for life. While still moving forward, when you look back and reflect on your journey, you gain both insight and a new perspective. Often, by paying attention to where you've been, you can learn some of life's most valuable lessons. My experience has been that if you don't pay attention and learn from lessons along the way, those life lessons tend to keep showing up until you do.

Take a moment to think about repeated struggles you've experienced in your life. Although the story and the characters may change, there is often a recurring theme. A mother I once worked with complained that friends and family often took advantage of her. She said she felt used because she was constantly serving others, yet they never returned the favor. One day, she said, "I seem to attract these people into my life!" What this mom didn't realize was she was being given the opportunity to learn to say no. Until she was aware of her own behavior, specifically the fear of saying no (because she didn't want to upset them), she would attract and be surrounded by people in her life who asked for her help. This mom learned the importance of saying no, and it wasn't long before her relationships began to get better. She was no longer afraid to say no, and her relationships with family and friends improved in ways she never could have imagined. Often, we don't reflect back on our lives until we're stuck—and don't know what else to do. Taking time each day to become aware of your emotions and behavior helps you become more proactive. Most importantly for a mom in the trenches, taking time to examine your life offers you the opportunity to make better choices.

As a mother of four adult children and grandmother of three, I often sit in the rear-facing seat of my life and look back. This helps me understand what's really important, what I could have let go of, and what I should have held onto. I understand better why my children sometimes said what they said, did what they did, or were confused by my confusion and lack of understanding. I am challenged to examine my way of being in the world, my actions and reactions, and the impact I have on others. If I could have a do-over as a parent, I would choose to reflect more often in the midst of the ups and downs of motherhood. Yet it's never too late!

The value of a reflective life is that you're able to make conscious choices and decisions based on past experiences. Self-reflection provides opportunities to determine what is or isn't working in a situation and figure out how to improve upon it. Through self-reflection, you're able to clarify what is important to you. Without knowing what really matters to you, how can you know what you want in life? Do you find yourself blindly going through life, just doing whatever is needed to survive the day? Once you gain clarity, you're able to live life with intention. Your life changes dramatically from survival mode (when you're doing what you can to just get through the day) to a life where you thrive because you're inspired to create positive changes daily.

A few years ago, I counseled a mother of two children, ages three and five. Larissa was a full-time mom with a full-time career. She called to schedule an appointment to discuss some of her parenting issues. The day she appeared in my office, Larissa quickly let me know how stressed she was. When I asked her what stressed her the most, she said, "Everything and everybody!" She explained that her days were full and long and that she had lost all patience, especially with her children. She told me that she was feeling guilty because that was not how she wanted to be as a mother. When she felt overwhelmed, she said, as hard as she tried not to, she often took it out on her kids.

"I want to spend more time with my children, but I never seem to find the time, which makes me feel even guiltier!"

When I asked her to describe how she spent her days, she quickly rattled off her to-do list, her deadlines, and her daily required activities (e.g., feed and bathe her children, take a shower, etc.).

I encouraged Larissa to take a moment and reflect on a time when she wasn't busy "doing" but was just "being." She looked at me with a blank stare. After a few moments, she remembered a time when one of her children was sick and sleeping in her arms. She said, "I remember just looking at her sweet face, and I felt calm in my heart." I asked Larissa if she was ever able to just be with her children, without an agenda or deadline, and she said no. She began to tear up and shared that she wasn't sure she even remembered *how* to be present with her children.

Typically when I work with parents, I recommend creating fifteen minutes of special time each day, but I sensed that having to find an additional fifteen minutes each day would add to Larissa's already excessive stress level. Instead, I recommended that Larissa find five minutes a day to think of as "special time"—time both she and her children could depend on. I also suggested she write her thoughts about her experience during that special time with her children in a journal and begin to reflect on her day and possible areas where she could carve out this dedicated time.

The following week, I saw Larissa again. When she walked in, I immediately noticed a difference in her energy. She seemed lighter and less burdened. Smiling, she exclaimed, "I'm loving my special time with my kids! When you initially suggested five minutes each day, I wasn't sure where I was going to find it, but I have since found twenty minutes!" When I asked her how she managed to do that, she shared that by examining her day and how her time was spent, she realized how much time she spent on her phone and computer. After reflection, Larissa decided that wasn't how she wanted to spend her time nor was it how she wanted her children to remember her as they grew up. She did not want to be a mom who was connected to her digital devices all the time!

She also said that since committing to the twenty-minute special time each day, both she and her children were much calmer. "And the best part is that I'm enjoying my children and being a mom again!" she said. During our first session, Larissa was very clear that she wanted to be a better mom, but she lacked clarity about how to achieve her goal. Larissa knew she wanted a better relationship with her children yet felt overwhelmed by her daily life. Think back to a time in your life when you were very clear about something you wanted. Perhaps you wanted to lose weight or learn a new skill. What did you need to get started? I know from experience that if I set a goal to lose five pounds but don't take a realistic look at myself and determine how I can purposefully achieve my goal, it's not going to happen. Asking myself "How is my current behavior going to support my goal?" begins the important internal conversation. When I reflect on my behavior and ask myself if I consistently eat mindfully (no) or go to the gym to exercise regularly (no, again), then I know that unless I change those behaviors, I have very little chance of achieving my desired goal.

Many of us set goals, but without taking the time to look at our own patterns of behavior, we don't achieve them. In an online article, author Allen R. McConnell writes, "Goals are a dime a dozen, but progress toward them requires an understanding of where we are now and how far away our ideals are from the present." He goes on to say, "Research in the psychological literature suggests that the negativity elicited from our awareness of a discrepancy between our current state and our goal is critical to spur self-improvement."[1]

Does this mean we have to experience negative emotions or consequences to make changes? Not necessarily, but negativity often motivates us to make changes. I've seen in my therapy practice that most parents don't reach out for help until they're in crisis. The negativity in the family has reached a tipping point, and they want things to change. It may be human nature to leave well enough alone until we're fed up or emotionally distraught, but I'm convinced that we don't have to wait for pain in order to make positive changes for ourselves or our families. There is a different way—a better way, I believe. Every day, we have a choice as to how we're going to show up in the world. When you pay attention and reflect on what is going on in your life and home, you're more apt to catch the problem before it leads to a crisis.

We have barometers and navigation systems that tell us when to correct our course. Our children, in particular, provide us daily opportunities to examine our own behavior and determine how we want to be both as a person and a mother. They can be our navigation system, if we take the time to notice. Their reactions to us help us to become more conscious of our choices. You have access to this information when you pay attention. Remember a time when you noticed the look on your child's face as you acknowledged their presence or listened carefully when they shared a story with you. Did they smile or become excited? Were they able to drop their defenses and be calm and at peace with you? Perhaps the more recognizable look might be when they felt unseen or unheard. Maybe you were in the middle of finishing a work project, checking one more email, or completely exhausted from your day, and your child's acting out seemed to spiral out of control. It was probably as if they were saying, "Please pay attention to me!" You've probably also seen that look as tears well up in their eyes: they look downward, sigh, or perhaps walk away in silence. Perhaps you've been so engrossed in what you were doing that you didn't notice the number of times they tried to talk to you.

We're all capable, as parents, of missing some moments because we are multitasking. However, when you're conscious and able to tap into their expression, you have the opportunity to look even closer, to clarify their feelings and reactions, and to determine what your contributing part might have been. This happens only when you're able to be present with your child.

When you pay attention, really pay attention, you're able to consciously choose the thoughts and behavior that best serve you and your child. You might decide to drop what you're doing and join your little one in their imaginative play. Maybe the laundry can wait just long enough for a quick game of Candyland. You are gifted many days with your children, many opportunities for inquiry and reflection—opportunities to really get to know your children and yourself. When you choose to take this journey consciously, you discover what really matters for both you and your family.

When you are present, committed, and openhearted, you have the ability to give your children the gift of wholeheartedness. This heart-filled gift—where you really see your children and connect with them at a deeper level—is priceless and has the potential to ripple out into the world. Imagine a world where we are no longer living on autopilot but are living with intention, in a heartfelt, connected way.

Most people do not practice self-reflection, especially not on a daily basis. Because of our busy lives, we are more apt to be unaware of our thoughts or behaviors in any given moment. Then something jolts us out of our complacency and we're forced to pay attention. Often, it's the loss of a job or a relationship challenge that forces us to stop and reassess our lives. Or we may be called to self-reflect not because of a crisis but because we sense a need for change. This may be a nagging feeling or an intuitive knowing that we need to take a closer look at our life. When this occurs, we're sometimes motivated to make changes, and other times, we fall back into our same old patterns. Change is hard. It's easy to distract ourselves and put self-reflection on the back burner.

I encourage you to take time to self-reflect, to gain clarity about yourself and your life. The Journaling Exercises below and throughout the book are designed to be beneficial no matter what stage of motherhood you are in. As you begin to take this journey, don't rush. The more time you spend with yourself, the greater your discoveries. The guided journal entries will help you dig deeper as you examine your thoughts and feelings. I remind you to do this without judgment. Be gentle with yourself and give yourself the gift of time—the time to know you, to discover what's important to you, and to decide how you want to live your life as a woman and a mother.

Live the questions now. Perhaps you will then gradually, without noticing it, live along some distant day into the answer.

—*Rainer Maria Rilke*, Letters to a Young Poet

Journaling Exercises

- ☺ Who were you before you were a mom?

- ☺ Before you were a mom, what got you excited, instilled you with passion, or provided a reason for you to jump out of bed in the morning?

- ☺ Do you still have that excitement? If not, where did it go?

- ☺ List three things that you loved to do as a child.

- ☺ Does thinking about any of these activities get you excited? Can you remember engaging in an activity in which you were unaware of how quickly time passed?

- ☺ Reflect on a time when you recently felt excited or full of joy. What were the circumstances? (For example, were you involved in an activity, spending time with a family member or friend, or perhaps relaxing at the beach?)

- ☺ Are you ready to rediscover what brings you joy? Is there anything stopping you?

- ☺ What three steps can you take to begin to bring joy back into your life? (Hint: Think about little ways to sprinkle joy throughout your day.)

- ☺ If you feel like you never have enough time, pay close attention to what is taking up your time. Write down those time-stealers. Ask yourself: what can be set aside or let go?

- ☺ After reading this chapter, knowing what I know now, I intend to . . .

Where Are You Now? Where Do You Want to Be?

As you journaled, were you able to tap into memories of yourself before you became a mother? Did you rediscover what excited you or brought you joy in the past? These are important first steps. It's difficult to make changes when you aren't sure what needs changing. But you have your own personal GPS navigation system at your disposal to help guide you. Your ability to self-reflect and listen to your own inner voice (yes, we all have an inner voice) is available to you at any time. Like the navigation voice saying "Recalculating," your inner voice can help remind you of the opportunity to try a different route, behavior, emotion, reaction, or response.

Making changes might not be easy—and often takes courage. As humans, it is our nature to strive for homeostasis and balance in our lives. We often feel more comfortable with the status quo. If letting go is difficult, consider examining yourself and your life through the lens of *Does this serve me or my child?* Then it becomes easier to let go, to see the bigger picture, and to determine what really matters. Like riding in the rear-facing seat of the car, when you look back and see where you've been, you have the opportunity to choose how you want to be now and where you want to go.

Chapter 2

Hopes, Wishes, and Dreams

All the art of living lies in a fine mingling
of letting go and holding on.

—Havelock Ellis

*H*ope helps create an optimistic future. Hope encourages you to keep going even when a situation seems hopeless. Hope promises a brighter future and reminds you that there are caring people in the world, in spite of what the daily news might show. Hope helps you endure uncertainty and tough times by encouraging you to maintain a positive focus.

Hope also helps guide you through your mothering journey. Mothers hope that their kids will grow up to be caring individuals, yet they understand that as they teach and model caring behaviors, they increase the likelihood that this will occur. Recently, a mother told me that when she first looked into her newborn son's eyes, she felt overwhelming hope that he would grow up to be a kind and compassionate young man. The mother explained it was this initial hope that provided her guidance as she raised her son. Hope provided a road map to help her consciously teach and instill the values she envisioned for her son.

Chapter Summary

As mothers, hopes and dreams allow us to hold onto our aspirations and vision for the future. We dream for ourselves and our children. The ability to hope carries all of us through the ups and downs of motherhood—through the sleepless nights, the terrible twos (or threes), and even our uncertainty about our ability to be a good mom. Sharing the importance of hopes and dreams with our children teaches them the value of envisioning all of life's possibilities. It teaches them the value of having their own aspirations and big dreams. Yet when we hold tight to our hopes and dreams—without taking time to examine them—they may easily become expectations. Expectations that limit our possibility and our child's. We have the opportunity to nurture our children and foster their growth as we learn to let go and allow them to reach their full potential. This is one of the best gifts we can give to our children.

I've heard people say that hope is naïve, a weakness, passive, or unrealistic. Recently, I was talking with a girlfriend about hope. She said she viewed hope as a weakness—as if just hoping for something to come true would automatically make it come true. She went on to say, "You have to take action in order for things to change. You can't just hope that it will." In her mind, hope was passive. I found this intriguing, because sometimes without hope, you're less likely to take action to move forward in the direction of what you hope will occur. But before becoming a mother, you probably had hope for yourself and for your child. That hope allowed you to focus on your desires as y ou began your journey into motherhood.

Dreams are actually created from seeds of hope. Hope can lead to a wish for something you desire. When that occurs, dreams begin to take form. And as you focus on your dream, giving it energy, you gain the impetus to take action toward making your dream a reality.

> The past is a source of knowledge, and the future is a source of hope.
>
> —Stephen Ambrose

The Reality of Your Dreams

As they anticipate the arrival of their babies, most (if not all) expectant mothers imagine themselves as mothers. You probably began to envision your baby from the moment you knew they were coming. How the baby came into your life really doesn't matter—whether from your own womb or through another's, you became a mother. And from that picture you created, you began to develop hopes and dreams for your child.

Those hopes and dreams began to take form as you imagined how motherhood would be before you were knee-deep in the trenches of caring for your children. Think back to a few of your hopes and dreams at that time. Were they similar or different from what they are now? Does your infant, child, or teen match what you had dreamed? Perhaps you saw a lighthearted and playful child or a shy youth like you. Maybe you imagined your son or daughter as athletic or artistic.

Before embarking on this journey, you may not have focused much on the difficulties of parenting—the temper tantrums, the daily messes that children create, or the long, sleepless nights. Jennifer Senior, author of *All Joy and No Fun: The Paradox of Modern Parenthood*, writes, "There's the parenting life of our fantasies, and there's the parenting life of our banal, on-the-ground realities."[2]

While reality can come close to your dreams, there are often surprising contrasts. No doubt before you became a mother, you observed other women with their children. I remember when I was pregnant with my first child, I saw a two-year-old melting down in the middle of a grocery store. His mother looked exasperated and helpless. I thought to myself smugly, "My child will *never* act that way!" Later, of course, I was that exasperated and helpless mother on many occasions.

Hope helps you navigate your way through difficult life circumstances. It helps you remember that nothing lasts forever. Hopes and dreams help you determine how you want to be a mother, in specific ways. They support you during your pregnancy as you anticipate and plan for the future while dreaming about how your life will change as your family expands. Young mothers often tell me that they were grateful for the time to plan and dream before they actually assumed the role of mother.

Mothers' dreams can influence the rules they create for their children and their own parenting style. This often occurs long before they are needed, yet it is valuable because its helps parents be more conscious in their parenting. When my daughter was eight months pregnant, she talked with me about the values she wanted to instill in her child. When making their plans, she and her husband had decided to limit the time they and their child would spend on digital devices. Although they could have waited until they were faced with the reality of digital devices, their earlier intention, created while awaiting the arrival of their baby, helped set the tone in their house and influenced their behavior as parents.

Katherine Wilson, author of the blog *Mummypinkwellies*, shared some of her hopes and dreams she had for her child:

- To love and be loved
- To never fear the future
- To choose the right way even when the right way is much harder
- To dare to be different and not afraid to be it
- To accept everyone for who they are and not judge
- To always know her parents love her, no matter what she does
- To take time out for herself when she needs to
- To be successful in anything she puts her mind to
- To not always listen to me (weird, I know, but I want her to learn to make her own decisions, and sometimes that means ignoring what others, including Mummy, say)
- To make mistakes, and learn from them[3]

> Hope begins in the dark, the stubborn hope that if you just show up and try to do the right thing, the dawn will come. You wait and watch and work: you don't give up.
>
> —*Anne Lamott*

Whether your hopes are for yourself or your family, they are beacons of light on your path. Mothers often tell me they hope their children will grow up to be responsible adults. Hope alone cannot guarantee their children's success as a young adult. However, a mother's hope leads her to take action in day-to-day mothering, such as teaching her child responsible behaviors and allowing him to experience the consequences of his choices.

I received a call from a disheartened mother, Kate, who stated her main goal as a mother was to raise a responsible son. Her voice lightened as she described how her fifteen-year-old was a gentle and responsible little boy. She shared many examples of his kindness and good manners. As Kate reminisced about a happier time with her son, she suddenly stopped. "What happened to my sweet little boy?" she asked. "I feel like someone abducted him and left me with a surly, mean-spirited young man." The prevailing question and concern in Kate's question about her son was *As a mother, where did I go wrong?* She was at a loss. Not only did she feel as if she'd lost her son as he once was, Kate said she had lost hope in her ability to parent him. What had worked before was no longer working. In fact, her tried-and-true parenting techniques only seemed to inflame the situation.

I acknowledged Kate's feelings and explained the normal developmental stages a child goes through from a toddler to a teen. Through our work together, Kate gained a better understanding of where her son was in his development. He no longer responded to her earlier way of parenting, so rather than try to manage her son's behavior, Kate learned to take on more of a consultant role. Kate became hopeful again as she learned new ways to parent her teen and saw positive results. Through this process, she learned to guide her son without micromanaging him. I encouraged Kate to hold onto her hope of raising a responsible young man in spite of what her son's ups and downs and outbursts might suggest. She learned to calm her anxiety and use her hopes and dreams as a guiding force. The rest was up to her son.

Recently, I saw Kate at a county park. She walked up to me and proudly announced that her eighteen-year-old had indeed turned out to be a fine young man. Kate felt the worst was behind them and that he was now making good choices for himself.

Hope does not guarantee a positive outcome, of course, but it helps sustain you in difficult times. Mothers have reported that after a miscarriage, it was hope that sustained them to attempt to become pregnant again. With the hope of conceiving and carrying a healthy baby to term, these women were able to move forward.

Most parents go through one incredible challenge or another with their children. One challenge, however, that could threaten to bury a parent's dream is illustrated in the story of a young couple anxiously awaiting the birth of their baby. Most parents eagerly await the arrival of their newborn, usually with anticipation and excitement. This particular couple, Allison and Dave, were anxious for a different reason. An early sonogram had alerted the obstetrician to possible health issues with the fetus. The parents were cautioned during the multiple sonograms to follow that their baby might not survive or else might live with birth defects. What kept this couple courageously moving forward on a daily basis was their hope that their infant would not only survive but also thrive; hope that the doctor was wrong; hope that the imaging had produced false results or incorrect information. By holding onto their hope, this couple refused to imagine the worst.

Finally, the day of their son's arrival came. Although there were congenital health issues, it was the parents' continued hope that sustained them as they faced the baby's future. Allison and Dave relied on their steadfast hope and continued to believe that because their son did survive, he would continue to grow and be healthy.

Journaling Exercises

Take time now to reflect on the hopes and dreams you held as you anticipated being a mother.

- Before I became a mom, I envisioned that my children would be . . .

- As I anticipated the arrival of my child, I envisioned myself as a mom to be . . .

- These hopes and dreams helped my child and me in the following ways:

Children Dream Big

Most children are hopeful by nature and have a natural ability to dream. They are very creative, and there is no limit to their imagination. Chances are your child is very good at creating wishes and dreams and most likely believes in them wholeheartedly. At a young age, it doesn't even occur to them that their wishes and dreams won't come true. Have you ever tried to talk a four-year-old out of his dream of becoming Spider-Man when he grows up?

A child's internal voice of doubt has not yet developed as it has in adults. Parents often view their child's dreams as whims and don't take them seriously. Your response can truly foster or hinder your child's dreams. As an adult, you may have your doubts about how realistic your child's dreams are, but why not support them and believe in the magic of their dreams? As their mother, if you believe in life's possibilities, you are in the perfect position to help foster their dreams and teach them how to reach their goals!

Successful people dream big. Some of them—like Bill Gates, Walt Disney, Albert Einstein, Stephen King, Oprah Winfrey, and Steven Spielberg—become famous. Others are known only to those whose lives they touch. They all have some things in common: a dream, belief in themselves, and a burning desire to achieve their dream against all odds. And, perhaps, a mother who believed in their dream, too.

Here are some ways to foster your child's dreams.

- ☯ Allow your child the freedom to dream
- ☯ Teach them life skills to live their dreams
- ☯ Expose them to many experiences, both educational and creative
- ☯ Encourage them to think outside the box . . . and color outside the lines
- ☯ Teach and model for them a positive worldview
- ☯ Encourage them to believe in their own dreams
- ☯ Send positive messages that you believe in their dreams

- ⚫ Teach them to take action
- ⚫ Show your support by letting your child know you have aspirations for them
- ⚫ Teach them that, even in failure, there are opportunities to reevaluate, redirect your course, or change your plan
- ⚫ Set a good example of overcoming obstacles
- ⚫ Always show your support[4]

These are abstract concepts, and you will find the best way to demonstrate your love, hope, and support, but here are a few specific things you can consider as you help your child cultivate hope.

- ⚫ Be a role model of hope for them
- ⚫ Share stories about how hope helped you maintain a positive attitude
- ⚫ Use the term hope in your everyday language
- ⚫ Acknowledge the importance of hope in your life; explain that hope helps you to face uncertainty and challenging situations
- ⚫ Remind them that each day is a new day and provides the opportunity to hope for a better tomorrow
- ⚫ Teach them that hope alone does not ensure their desired outcome

Children, who are not naturally hopeful, can benefit from being taught how to incorporate hope into their lives. And it's essential for our children to be hopeful. Research suggests that, although it takes time, helping children cultivate hope provides significant rewards for the kids. According to Vicki Zakrzewski, PhD, the education director of the Greater Good Science Center, "Researchers have found that students who are high in hope have greater academic success, stronger friendships, and demonstrate more creativity and better problem-solving. They also have lower levels of depression and anxiety and are less likely to drop out from school."[5]

A hopeful child sees life's possibilities. They often believe that anything is possible, and it's up to us as parents to help foster their hopes and dreams. A child who is hopeful is motivated to work hard in order to pursue her dreams, to maintain her focus on the work necessary to chase her dreams.

That being said, it's equally important to teach your child that hope is more than wishful thinking and that it requires motivation and action on their part. For example, when your teen hopes to make the football team but doesn't take steps to improve his skills, he may learn that hope takes him only so far. You can teach your child to set goals based on his or her hopes and then identify action steps to help them attain the goal. You can also help them brainstorm various ways to achieve their goal. So if your teenager dreams of being an actress, perhaps you can help her sign up for drama classes or work with a drama coach. Remind your child that pursuing a dream takes passion, practice, and patience.

As important as it is to support your child in their many dreams, it's also important to help them consciously choose what dreams they want to hold onto and which ones they would like to let go. Sometimes children—like adults—hold onto dreams from their childhood and have a difficult time letting them go. They may also hold onto a particular dream for the parent's sake.

Zachary, a seventeen-year-old, dreamed of being an astronaut since the age of four. Although Zachary continued to hold onto his dream, he struggled in science and math. Zachary had received extra support from his teachers and spent many hours with tutors, but he continued to fall behind in math and science. He began to realize that he may not be able to fulfill his dream. Zachary understood that his low scores in math and science would prohibit him from having the qualifications needed to become an astronaut. Although he was disappointed to let go of his childhood dream, Zachary began to pursue other interestes with the support of his parents.

Your son or daughter may have lost interest in their pursuit yet found another career path they're equally passionate about. As their parent, you're able to guide them as they learn to alter their dreams to fit what works best for their life. This skill to revise what once was a dream will be valuable to them throughout time. Revisiting dreams is a lifelong process.

When to Let Go of Dreams

Hopes and dreams are beneficial when they're rooted in reality. When you closely examine the reality of your hopes and dreams, you may discover that some don't match your current situation. Seeing the difference allows you to decide which dreams to hold onto and move toward and which to let go. Sometimes, as a mom, it's not easy to let go of long-held dreams—and it may take courage to let go of what no longer fits. However, holding onto a long-held dream that doesn't match your current reality may not serve you or your child.

I worked with Jill, a mother who dreamed her daughter would follow the family tradition of being a schoolteacher. When she was young, Amber loved to play school, especially when she took on the role as teacher. For years, Jill thought her dream for Amber was coming true. One day, her daughter, now headed for college, announced she was going to major in horticulture. Jill was crushed. Eventually, she realized she had assumed her daughter would become a teacher but had never actually asked Amber about *her* dreams. It's vital to realize that your hopes and dreams for your children can be beneficial—but only if held lightly. If held with a heavy hand, your hopes and dreams can lead to heartache and potential resentment if your dreams don't fit your child's.

As mothers, we often create dreams for our children, but then the lines become blurred when we believe our dreams are actually our child's dreams. Try to recognize that perhaps your dreams for your child aren't as much for your child but rather more for yourself. When you project your own dreams onto your child, you rob them of their ability to dream—for themselves. Living vicariously through your child doesn't allow them to live their own life, nor do you live your own. Of course, you may be disappointed that your son or daughter did not realize the dream you'd hoped for them, but the reality is, this is *their life to live*. Let your kids have the freedom to live their own life, and enjoy living your own.

Sometimes it's difficult to distinguish your dream from reality. I get it. This is the first step that will increase your ability to decide what's worth holding onto and what you should let go of. This is where discernment comes in. In order to be clear about which dreams are worth holding onto, have the courage to be honest with yourself about what fits reality and what doesn't. It's a weeding-out process, and it can be done only after you've closely examined the origin of your dream.

Your hopes and dreams are often based on your preconceived notions. According to *Merriam-Webster*, a preconceived notion is an idea or opinion "form[ed] prior to actual knowledge or experience."[6] In other words, preconceived notions are predetermined—but on what basis? Think back to a preconceived notion you had about your child, perhaps when you were pregnant. At the time, you may have felt confident in your idea. You may, as I did, have developed a preconceived notion that children who misbehave out in public do so as a result of poor parenting. Your assumption, based on that notion, may not be true.

However, based on your unfounded notion, you may automatically assume your child will be well behaved because you'll be a better parent. What happens, then, when your child misbehaves? And he or she will. Your preconceived notion may lead you to believe you've failed as a parent. Each time your child acts out (and it's inevitable), you have proof that you've failed as a parent. This false belief most likely will encourage you to exert more control over your child in an attempt to get them to behave. Please understand that, contrary to your own notion, your child's behavior is not a reflection of your poor parenting ability. Your misguided perception that blames parents for their child's behavior has been a bit askew. This is just one risk of holding onto hopes and dreams that are based on unsubstantiated preconceived ideas.

Preconceived notions can also lead to expectations. Some parents assume a child's temperament will continue into adulthood, but that expectation denies these kids from ever having the chance to show their true essence—who they really are. For example, picture the father who envisions his baby boy becoming a pro football player. Maybe he's got a photo of his newborn with a football in the bassinet. As the little one grows, so does the dad's dream. The father plans his son's activities and gifts around football. Fast-forward to when the boy is eight years old. His father has signed him up for football, even though the boy clearly doesn't enjoy the sport. He resists Saturday morning practice and finds excuses to avoid playing football with his dad in the backyard. The father doesn't give up, though. He rationalizes that his son will learn to love the game. Now fast-forward again to when his son starts high school. Once again, the dad encourages his son to try out for the football team. He expects him to join. Whatever decision is made about football, someone will be unhappy and perhaps resentful. Many teens have told me that the only reason they play sports or take dance lessons, for example, is because they feel they have to in order to gain their parent's approval or avoid their anger or disappointment. I've worked with several teens with college sports scholarships who suddenly refuse to continue playing the sport. Why? Often because the parent's preconceived notions and expectations didn't take the child's wishes into consideration. The parent's wishes didn't align with the child's desires.

Preconceived notions can easily turn into unrealistic expectations. There is greater energy, often negative, devoted to expectations. This negative energy stems from your need to hold onto or cling to what you believe is best.

Expectations were like fine pottery. The harder you held them, the more likely they were to crack.

—*Brandon Sanderson*, The Way of Kings

Some mothers expend a lot of energy wanting things to be different than they are. Wanting something to be different than it is can lead to an attempt to control your kids and also creates a lot of suffering. Can you think of a time when you wanted something to be different? You were convinced that "if only" this situation were different, or this person acted differently, all would be well. Tory, a mother I met with, told me that she was upset at the beginning of the school year when her daughter, Molly, was put in the wrong classroom. What she was specifically talking about was that her daughter was assigned to the "wrong" teacher. Molly's sensitivity was a sharp contrast to her teacher's assertive nature, and Tory was convinced her daughter would suffer in school. Tory felt that the teacher wouldn't understand her daughter and wouldn't be able to give Molly the caring support she needed. Tory went to great lengths to get her daughter moved to a different class. The school was resistant, yet Tory held firm. The mother's frustration and failed attempts began to consume her time and emotional energy. Meanwhile, although Molly was initially intimidated by her teacher's assertive nature, she also began to observe her teacher's kindness. Each time the teacher took time to acknowledge a student or share a story, the little girl noticed. With her teacher's support, Molly learned to let down her guard and began asserting herself in the classroom. The reality was this little girl didn't want another teacher. When she shared her feelings with her mother, Tory realized that her little girl wasn't suffering at school. In fact, she loved school and was doing quite well. Tory had created her own suffering by firmly holding onto wanting things to be different than they were, and she realized it was time to let go.

Suffering usually relates to wanting things
to be different from the way they are.

—*Allan Lokos*, Pocket Peace: Effective Practices for
Enlightened Living

Another risk of dreams and wishes is that when you are attached to wanting circumstances to be different than they are, you're usually not able to see reality. You cling to an idea about how things should be, which can create unnecessary suffering. Holding onto attachments can be mentally and physically exhausting and can create disappointment for you and your family. And when you're not willing to let go, you may resort to control with potentially harmful effects. Is it easy to let go of unrealistic expectations? It depends how long you've been holding onto them and how attached you are to them.

Expectations are often rooted in the stories we tell ourselves. Brené Brown, renowned research social worker and best-selling author, encourages people to explore and examine their own stories. Like many others, she finds that people are "wired for story." However, she writes, "A lot of the stories we tell ourselves just aren't true."[7] She urges us to examine our stories and our truth as we see it. When you take the time to examine your own hopes and dreams and the associated stories you've told yourself, you then have the opportunity to hold onto what is true and let go of what no longer serves your children or yourself.

Journaling Exercises

- Think back to a situation in which you felt that someone, perhaps one of your parents, had unrealistic expectations of you. Expectations designed to fulfill their own needs—not yours. How did you feel about their expectations?

- How did this affect you?

- Have you had dreams for your children that didn't align with their own?

- What hopes and dreams have you had to let go?

🕊   How difficult was it to let them go?

🕊   What hopes and dreams have you held onto that have begun
      to materialize? How did you feel when they came true?

🕊   What was different about the dreams that didn't happen? Did
      your actions support your dreams?

🕊   Reflect on your own capability to support your child's ability
      to dream. How do you do this? When you do, how does your
      child respond?

The Freedom of Reality

Seeing the truth, the reality of what is, can be freeing, although it may
feel scary. I've listened to mothers talk about their fear related to looking at their own truth. When I've asked them what they fear, some
say they're afraid they'll uncover something they don't want to see.
For example, some mothers fear that the truth is they don't want to
be married anymore. Others are afraid they may find out they don't
want to be a mother. No matter what the truth is, every mother I've
worked with who has had the courage (and yes, it does take courage)
to face reality has found it freeing. They are less guarded, less judgmental, and more accepting of all of their feelings.

Most mothers discover they're overwhelmed as a wife and mother not because they don't want to be in that role but simply because
they need more help and more time for themselves. They often find
that what they're really experiencing is a sense of losing themselves in
marriage and motherhood. When your hidden feelings are allowed to
see the light of day, your truth can actually free you.

Glennon Doyle Melton, founder of the blog *Momastery*, has
mastered the art of truth-telling for moms. In fact, she has inspired
a social movement to support mothers and put truth-telling on the
map (something that many mothers have not felt comfortable doing

due to fear of being judged)—to be honest and bold while letting go of feelings of unworthiness and imperfection. She invites mothers "to believe in themselves, to be brave and kind, to let go of the idea of perfection, and to stop making motherhood, marriage, and friendship harder by pretending they're not hard."[8]

By letting go of perfection, which often stems from unrealistically high expectations of yourself and others, you allow room for the truth of what is. Think back to a time when you wanted life to be different than it was (the truth of what is) and spent a lot of energy pretending that it was something different (not truth-telling). For example, a mother once told me that she felt her whole life was a lie. She explained that because her childhood was often chaotic and unstable, she tried to make sure her life was filled with certainty. She carried this need for certainty into marriage and motherhood. She was unrelenting in her attempts to control her spouse's decisions, her children's behavior, and her family's circumstances. Her fear of letting go, while learning to trust and accept what was, caused her to hold firmly in an attempt to keep life orderly. Her house needed to be in "perfect" order each day, as did her children's appearance and behavior.

This mother's fear was not only holding herself and others hostage, but it was also exhausting. Through her own self-work, she learned to loosen her grasp and let go of her need for control. What she discovered as a result was the freedom to live life with more ease. Once she no longer tried to control her husband and children, they too began to relax.

When you give yourself permission to see things as they are, you experience a more relaxed way of being. Your interactions with others become more enjoyable because you no longer feel the need to be in control. And you regain all the energy you spent pretending. It doesn't take much energy to accept what is, even when it's unpleasant.

The ability to face the truth, however, doesn't happen automatically. It takes practice. But it's a practice worth cultivating. I have a small plaque in my kitchen that reads *It is what it is*. Each day, I look at it and am reminded that when I want things to be different than they are, I create my own suffering. Holding onto my expectations and inability to see the truth for what it is only adds to my own discomfort.

Kathryn Schulz, journalist, author, and TED talk speaker, states, "The miracle of your mind isn't that you can see the world as it is. It's that you can see the world as it isn't."[9] She explains that we're often not only wrong—we're unaware of how wrong we are. Reality is filtered through one's own perceptions and biases, which often results in distortion—a distortion one believes is true and holds onto for a long time. Fractured relationships are often a result of distortions. Based on misperceptions and biases, people easily judge and disconnect from one another. As a mother, you have the ability and responsibility to be consciously aware of the truth you're creating. By having the courage to examine your truths, you're able to decide what fits reality and what you should let go of. This doesn't mean you condone or support what may be present for you (what you observe) but that you can become more mindful in how you respond to the situation.[10]

Shawn Achor, *New York Times* bestselling author of *Before Happiness* (2013) and *The Happiness Advantage* (2010), states, "Ninety percent of your long-term happiness is predicted not by the external world but by the way your brain processes the world." Your perception of "what is" and your associated feelings have a direct influence on your own happiness. The maxim *The truth will set you free* may not be true if your truth is distorted.[11]

You may develop unrealistic expectations based on your distortions of truth for yourself and your child. But truth allows you to see the joys and difficulties of motherhood. Holding the juxtaposition of both—*and*, not *or*—is truth-telling and freeing. Seeing your children for who they are or how they're being in the moment allows them to grow into who they are and who they're becoming—and it allows you to enjoy that reality.

Truth deepens the connection between a mother and child. Once you drop your need for control and let go of long-held unrealistic expectations, life's possibilities begin to appear. Remember that expectations built on your truth, not necessarily that of your child's, can hinder, rather than foster, your child's growth. Expectations that stem from an accurate truth can actually help the growth of an individual. Expecting your child to do their best in school is different from expecting your child to get straight As in school. And you're able to help guide them as they discover for themselves what their best is.

It takes courage to look at the truth. Through a lens that allows you to see and honor your child for who they are. To acknowledge and celebrate their dreams—even if they differ from your own.

Journaling Exercises

Knowing what you now know, what are you willing to let go of? Take the opportunity now to examine your own hopes and dreams that may not be serving you or your family.

- What hopes and dreams have you had to let go of in the past (these may include those before you became a mom)?

- How hard was it to let go?

- What hopes, wishes, or dreams have you held onto that you're afraid to look at? What are you afraid to let go of?

- How would your life change if you were willing to look at the truth?

- After reflecting upon your hopes, wishes, and dreams, what have you discovered? Would you change any of them? If so, which ones?

- How would dreaming with your child change your relationship?

- Knowing what I know now, I intend to . . .

When you're able to loosen your grip on what you have held onto so tightly, you create space for other possibilities. Through this process, you allow yourself to examine and dream of life in a different way—perhaps a clearer way.

Chapter 3

Can You See Clearly?

The greatest potential we have for opening our hearts lies in the opening of our minds.

—Vironika Tugaleva, *The Love Mindset*

*Y*ou have a choice, each day, in how you see the world. You can choose to see a situation or individual with kindness or judgment. It's your choice. Your lens is influenced by past experiences, but you can allow or reject how your experiences may color your perspective. This moment-to-moment decision is often one we aren't even aware of, though more often, we're acutely aware of each other's. Can you remember a time when you felt uncomfortable as you watched someone berate another individual? Belittle them in a way that was painful to watch? As difficult as it may seem, the individual or group who vehemently criticizes others is in pain. The internal lens through which they view others has been clouded or distorted.

As women and as mothers, it is important for us to be aware of our lens and how our experience has created our unique perceptions. Have you ever stopped to consider how you view your world?

Chapter Summary

Have you considered how your lens or outlook has impacted your relationship with yourself? With your children? Most of us view the world through our particular lens, unaware of the extent to which it determines what we see—a lens created from past experiences and distorted messages we've received along the way. It is only when we see the world with soft eyes, eyes full of compassion and acceptance, that we find understanding.

Seeing clearly with soft eyes allows you to drop unconscious assumptions and judgments, to delve beneath your perceptions and attachments and open yourself to the truth of who your children are, not who you think they should be.

A clearer understanding helps you nurture whole-hearted and authentic relationships. It begins by seeing yourself with acceptance and love. And it culminates when you can see your children, truly see them—not for their misbehavior, but for their true essence—and the miracle that they are in your life.

When you're able to drop your filter and fully open your eyes, that's when you begin to see reality. Facing reality, rather than seeing it the way you want it to be, allows you to see the truth. When you begin to see things more clearly, you're able to handle even the most difficult situation. It's also when you're truly able to be authentic in your relationship with your child.

> An open mind is also a humble mind because it realizes how little it actually knows.
>
> —*Russell Anthony Gibbs*, The Six Principles of Enlightenment and Meaning of Life

Seeing Yourself

I was recently fitted for contact lenses. The eye doctor discussed hard versus soft lenses. I left her office and thought about how we each have the capability of viewing life through either a hard or soft lens. Metaphorically, when seeing through a hard lens, it's easy to assume you know or have a clear understanding of a particular situation—tunnel vision. Whereas when you're willing to look through a soft lens, you allow more room for curiosity and possibility. You're then given the opportunity to see someone or a situation from a wider view or different perspective. Softer eyes or lenses encourage us all to see people and life in a different and better way with understanding and compassion.

Too often, women and mothers turn those hard lenses inward, criticizing themselves for appearance, failures, and omissions. We berate and plague ourselves with guilt, seeing only through the hard lenses of our own (perhaps unrealistic) expectations.

As a mother, you have your own individual way of seeing the world—viewed through your internal lens of experiences and hopes. Do you belittle yourself when you fall short? Chances are your perceptions of and relationships with your children vary, not only because of who they are but also because of who you are. Most mothers, when honest with themselves, admit to connecting with one of their children more or differently than another. This is often hard for mothers to admit without feeling guilty. Perhaps you've experienced this yourself. Although you love all your children, you may connect and relate to one more easily than others. That's the truth, and there is absolutely nothing to feel guilty about. It's very normal to relate to some of your kids differently than others. Chances are you find it easier to parent the child you feel more connected to. If you have only one child and have a difficult time relating or connecting with them, you may struggle and wonder why.

Remember: it's human nature to connect with those who are similar. You've probably experienced this with friends in your life. In your circle of girlfriends, do you find there are those who you connect with more easily than others? You might enjoy all of your girlfriends' company, but you prefer to spend more time with those who are more similar to you. It's also natural to avoid those who mirror characteristics that you don't like about yourself. The same is true with all relationships in your life, including (or especially) with your children.

Besides recognizing similarities between yourself and others, you also see others through your personal lens. For example, your child's behavior may trigger you because his or her behavior reminds you of someone from your past. Perhaps your knee-jerk reaction to your child's incessant whining or angry outburst reminds you of someone who also pushes your buttons. Recently, a mom in my parenting class had an *aha* moment when she realized her son's lack of respect for her triggered her memories of her father's lack of respect for her. Are you able to be curious, without judgment, about why your buttons are so easily pushed? I remind parents that their buttons are being pushed for a reason—and, most likely, they stem from the parents' own unresolved issues, experiences and emotions that they've buried and perhaps have long forgotten. When you are triggered by your child's behavior, it might be time to look a little deeper.

Can you see yourself with soft, gentle eyes? When you look at yourself in the mirror or in a photo, who do you see? Are you able to look at yourself, really look at yourself, without any preconceived ideas or judgments?

Many moms and women I know spend more time focusing on their faults, often unconsciously, and very little time really looking at themselves, gently, with soft eyes. It isn't uncommon to hear women complain: "My hair is too flat; my eyes are too puffy; this photograph makes me look fat," and on and on they go. You too may quickly look away from your own photo or concentrate on certain aspects that you don't like about yourself. On the other hand, some women are very comfortable in front of the camera.

A few years ago, I read Carl Studna's beautiful book, *Click!: Choosing Love One Frame at a Time.* Studna, who has photographed the likes of Paul McCartney, Marianne Williamson, Deepak Chopra, and the Dalai Lama, explains that some people are more self-conscious than others and then asks, "Is being self-conscious a bad thing?" He breaks down the word *self-conscious* and states that "it simply means to be conscious of one's self." Studna defines it as "being aware of one's way of thinking, speaking, acting, and overall way of being."[12] Something we all might benefit from, right? Sure—to a point.

When we allow our ego to rule our thoughts and beliefs, we can easily slip into judgment. That is the moment in time when our ability to see with soft eyes is clearly diminished. How often do you pick apart photos of others as much as you do yourself? Probably not very often, but we women are often our own worst critics! Do you celebrate what you're able to do or criticize your abilities? When was the last time you patted yourself on the back for doing a good job? Can you even remember?

Imagine how your day, your life, might be different if you were able to see yourself through soft, gentle eyes, accepting yourself as is. When you consciously acknowledge what you're doing right (I promise you— there are many things you're doing right) instead of berating yourself for what you're doing wrong. How might your life change when you begin to focus on and celebrate your own goodness. Kathryn Thompson, author of *Drops of Awesome*, encourages moms to honor and embrace themselves fully. She states, "*Drops of Awesome* is really about allowing yourself to feel joy and to be proud of your small victories."[13] Think of the gifts you'd receive (love, acceptance, and nonjudgment, to name a few) simply by gifting yourself some drops of awesome. When you begin to see yourself with soft eyes, learn to be gentle with yourself, and love yourself for who you are, the gifts are endless.

Self-love begins by recognizing your goodness—honoring yourself for who you are in this moment. Just as your children aren't perfect, neither are you. Instead of beating yourself up for what you think you're not doing right, congratulate yourself for what you are doing right. It's easy to be overly critical, and it seems that when we enter motherhood, we inevitably raise the bar—and our own expectations. As if being "good enough" on our own was all right but can't be tolerated as a mother.

The phrase *good-enough mother* was coined to relieve mothers of their burden of never being good enough. But when is enough good enough? How will a mother know? And why is one mother's "good enough" not good enough in the eyes of other mothers? The guilt that mothers engender can easily become a way of life if left unexamined and untethered.

Like I mentioned earlier, mama guilt plagues many mothers. The feelings that you're not a good-enough mother or that you will never measure up to other mothers only feeds your guilt. "Mother's guilt" is the gift no one wants that keeps on giving! It can drag you down, can make you doubt yourself, and is never productive. I promise you, there's absolutely nothing about holding onto negative feelings of guilt that will serve you as a mother.

If there is something you do as a mother that you feel is unhealthy or impacts your child negatively, I encourage you to explore your motives. Don't live with the guilt; change what you are doing! If you live in a guilt-ridden state because you constantly disappoint your child by not following through on your promises, then it's probably time to look at what's keeping you from honoring your promise. And if you're suffering from mama guilt because you continuously lose your temper with your child, that could be a wake-up call to some underlying frustration and anger you might be harboring. Only allow guilt in long enough to recognize why it's there;

don't let it hang around to weigh you down. And when you let go of your guilt, you make space to see the good in you and learn to value your uniqueness.

Journaling Exercises

When you learn to value yourself, it's natural for you to begin to see the value in others. Are you ready to discover the goodness within you? Take some time to complete the following journaling exercises.

- Do you see yourself through a soft or hard lens?

- When was the last time you complimented yourself? Name one or two things that you like or love about yourself—I bet once you begin, you'll find a few more!

- Now name something you don't like about yourself that you're willing to let go of or change.

- List two things that you believe you do right; you get to decide what "right" is for you.

- List two things related to motherhood that make you feel you're doing really well.

- It's easy to focus on what you're doing wrong—but this is a waste of your energy and time. Is there anything that you're feeling guilty about? Are there any particular actions you can take to lessen your guilt (something that you can do differently to change what you're feeling guilty about)?

Seeing Others with Soft Eyes

When you look at those around you, are you able to see them with soft eyes? With gentle, compassionate eyes that seek to understand

and accept rather than assume? Or do you view them through critical eyes, hardened by past experience? It's human nature to think we
already "know" them, to be quick to judge. We make assumptions,
especially with our children. How many times have you looked at
your children, assuming you know how they are feeling or what their
behavior actually means? Your assumptions are most likely based on
the past. Each time your child melts down, you may assume it's because they're not getting their own way. It's natural that you would
assume this if every time you say no to your child, they have a meltdown. Although you might be right, you might also be wrong—or at
least inaccurate—in your assumption.

Repetitive patterns and learned behavior begin to develop between every child and parent, and they become rigid if the parent's
lens is rigid as well. For example, take Zoe, a determined little four-
year-old who became angry each time her parents told her no. I began
to work with Zoe, at her parents' request, to help her calm herself and
manage her emotions. Fairly quickly, I determined that Zoe reacted
not as much from hearing the word no but more out of not feeling
heard. Even at her young age, she recognized that her parents could
not always say yes, but as soon as she heard no, along with all the
reasons why the answer was no, she felt powerless. She had a difficult
time understanding why her parents wouldn't listen to how she felt.
This wise little girl wanted to be heard.

Once I explained this to Zoe's parents, they were able to shift their
own lens and see the situation from Zoe's perspective. Their willingness to soften their lens gave them the foundation to help Zoe in the
way that she needed. Through my work with Zoe, she learned that
although the answer might still be no to her request to have a playdate that day, the answer most likely would be yes if a plan was made
to schedule it for another day. Through this process, Zoe learned to
delay her need for instant gratification (an immediate playdate) and
felt empowered to express her desires in a healthy way. Zoe's parents
learned not to assume that Zoe's meltdowns were always just because
she was told no. They began to understand the real reason behind

the behavior and were able to acknowledge her disappointment while helping her express her feelings. Through her parents' help, Zoe learned to problem-solve and take responsibility for her own feelings and behavior.

Soft eyes allow you to look deeper. Critical or judgmental eyes often allow you to see things only superficially, without taking the time to delve deeper. When you're quick to judge, you're seeing with critical eyes. Seeing your children with judgment or criticism clouds your vision and decreases the odds of seeing them fully for who they are. When a child says, "You always think I'm bad," they may feel they're the one who's often blamed first when something happens in the family. Perhaps when you hear a cry from your youngest daughter, you assume that your eight-year-old daughter is to blame. You come running into the room and start yelling, never thinking to ask what happened. Or if your son tells you, "You always say I'm lazy when I forget to do my homework. I'm not lazy, but sometimes I have a hard time keeping everything straight in my mind." Have you ever stopped to think, dig deep, and ask yourself if perhaps your child is right? Maybe you have made assumptions.

If you have young children and haven't experienced these types of exchanges with them (yet), you may remember feeling frustrated with your own parents when they were quick to criticize your behavior. Were there times when you felt that your parents made inaccurate assumptions about your behavior and then created broad generalizations that weren't true? It's easy to fall into a pattern of judgment when you view others through a critical eye and assume you know. What you create from judgment and believe to be true may actually become a self-fulfilling prophecy. What you focus on may indeed grow.

I've worked with many children who have given up trying to improve their conduct because, in spite of their efforts, they witness their parents continuing to focus on their negative behavior. They feel that their parents rarely acknowledge what they've done right and continue to point out what they've done wrong. When working with children and teens to help them improve their behavior (which definitely could use improvement), they often tell me, "It doesn't matter what I do. My parents are going to blame me anyway. They never see what I do right!"

This blame and shame surrounding the child's behavior is destructive and does not empower children to learn from their mistakes. Nor does it teach children the importance of making appropriate decisions in the future. As long as they feel they can do no right in the eyes of their parents and others, chances are they will continue to do wrong. When you're able to see your children with soft eyes, with a curiosity about why they might be doing what they're doing, you begin to experience a shift in your own way of seeing them. Your ability to do so will help you change your way of being with them.

You always have the opportunity to choose a different perspective, a new way of seeing, to help you find creative ways to guide your children. Recently, a single mom told me that her son was not willing to learn new skills. She was specifically referring to her son's resistance to learning to ride his new bike. This mom and her son had many struggles related to her trying to help her son learn (school assignments, piano, bike riding). As a result, she made the assumption that this was a problem he had. One day, a neighbor offered to help teach her son to ride his bike. The mom observed that he was more willing to listen to the neighbor than he had been to her. He dropped his resistance, and within a short period of time, he was bike riding with his friends in the neighborhood. This mom took a moment to soften her eyes and see her "teaching moments" from her son's perspective. When she did, she realized that her own frustration and anxiety were probably influencing her child's resistance. Her new perspective allowed her to change her own way of teaching her child—she chose to be more playful and less controlling and welcomed the support of other parents who were willing to also help teach her child.

Maybe you and your child don't struggle with resistance—but quite the opposite. Another mother complained that her five-year-old daughter was constantly seeking attention from her. I explained that children want attention and will seek both positive and negative attention. I also explained that even though she spent a lot of time with her daughter, much of the time it was focused on taking her daughter places or ensuring that she had brushed her teeth, straightened up her toys, or was getting ready for bed. I suggested she spend time playing with her daughter. The mother exclaimed, "All she wants to do is play princess, and I don't know how to play princess." I assured her that her daughter would let her know if she was doing it wrong.

Spending special time with your child lets them know that they're important—that they matter. Children feel seen and heard when you are present with them. Your "in the moment" time periods may be only five or ten minutes, but if your intention is to honor your child by spending time with them, your mission will be accomplished. Of course, your child will want to extend the time, and you can let them know you would like more time, too! If you have another commitment, remind your child that you love spending time with them and look forward to your next special time together. Don't forget to schedule special time. Put it on the calendar and remind your child that you're excited to see what you do next time. Allow your child to pick the activity. I advise mothers to spend time enjoying their children without feeling the need to teach or direct their child in any way, to simply see their child and observe their way of being in the world. I instruct mothers to be mindful of their own thoughts, preconceived notions, and judgments. To see their child through soft eyes. After doing this, many mothers have told me that they are now able to see their children in a more loving way. They recognize that their child is more than their behavior.

It's true, however, that even when we slow down and try to have special time with children, we may have a child that can push our buttons, spoiling our efforts to see them with soft eyes. I've worked with several mothers who were easily triggered by their sons' angry outbursts. What these mothers had in common was their automatic reaction to their sons' anger. They automatically assumed that their son was "just like his father" and exhibited the exact same anger issues.

They were also quick to assume they had either learned the behavior or inherited the temperament from their father. After spending time exploring their frustration, these mothers discovered that the underlying issue was with their own frustration with their husband, not their child.

Lisa, a single mother of two, consulted with me about her ten-year-old son's angry outbursts. Within a few minutes of our first meeting, Lisa stated in an exasperated tone, "He's just like his father—and that's why I divorced him. I was sick and tired of his anger and didn't want to expose myself or my kids to it anymore!" She further explained that each time her son, Alex, became angry, her chest tightened and she wanted to flee. Because of Lisa's past experience with her ex-husband, she saw her son through the same lens. Until Lisa became aware of her distorted lens, there was little chance that she'd be able to look at Alex's behavior from a different perspective. A different lens helped her connect with her son and allowed him to explore and express his feelings in a healthy manner.

Often, when our children trigger a reaction from us, it's not the child's behavior that is the issue. The real issue is that our eyes are conditioned by some experience that causes us to see a distorted reality. Softened eyes can look inward to discover the cause of the trigger, without judgement. You're capable of choosing to examine and resolve the issue. And yes, it is a choice. After taking the time to do this, you're then able to look outward and have a better understanding of your child, who unknowingly stepped on a landmine.

I certainly had triggers that my children stumbled upon, but I was also prone to wearing rose-colored glasses, the magical lens that helped me look at situations in a favorable light. Sometimes mothers do this to protect themselves from looking at reality. Rose-colored glasses can help you get through a situation when it's too painful to look at. They become lenses used to protect yourself. Maybe you've done this in your life. As a young child, I certainly I did. I wore those glasses for most of my childhood. Those glasses protected me when life was too harsh to look at with a clear lens.

Based on my own painful childhood, I decided my children wouldn't suffer as I had. I'd already determined that if you loved your children, it'd be more than enough. I envisioned my life as a mom, and it had a beautiful glow to it. I envisioned myself as a loving, kind, and patient mother. But my rose-colored glasses didn't always serve us, as the lens prevented me from accepting all that motherhood had to offer—not only the good (awesomeness) but also the bad (the tough days) and the ugly (when you weren't sure how you were going to survive).

Before becoming a mother, did you ever watch a teenager talk to their parent in a disrespectful manner? You may have thought to yourself, as I did, "My teen will never disrespect me like that." If so, you too may have a tendency to wear rose-colored glasses. If you're currently a mom of a teenager or have raised a teenager, you can relate. I was one of those moms. Don't get me wrong: my children were loving, kind, and patient. They also became angry at times and weren't always kind on the surface—just as there were times I wasn't kind on the surface. I wish for all our sakes I'd taken those glasses off more often.

Accepting all the aspects of motherhood and each of the facets of our children, with lenses free from clouding, distortion, and rosy tints, frees you to keep your vision flexible and accepting. It liberates you and your family from assumptions and expectations, from judgment and anxiety.

Seeing Your Child

When you're critical of yourself, it's very easy to be critical of others, especially your children. There may be days when you feel overwhelmed, as most mothers do. I often hear mothers lament that most of the time they spend with their children seems to be focused around just trying to get through daily tasks like mealtime, household chores, and homework, not to mention bedtime. Some mothers have told me that as they fall into bed at night, they often wonder if they looked at their child, really looked at them. Seeing your children, really "seeing" them, as obvious as that sounds, may not be at the top of your to-do list. How often do you actually take the time to see them without focusing on the task at hand? You're likely thinking about what needs to get done or how things should have been done. It's like looking through dirty glasses, unable to see the beauty through the grime.

Many mothers tell me that when they discuss with their child what needs to get done, they rarely look at them. Often mothers call to their children in the other room to remind them to get ready for bed—not because they're bad or neglectful mothers, just very busy mothers doing the best they can. I believe we're all doing the best we can at that moment until we wake up and learn how we can do better.

How many times have you found yourself looking at your child as they enter the room only to notice their dirty face or their clothes that are mismatched? Or perhaps you're still stewing about their recent failing grade on their report card. It is easy to focus on what is wrong rather than what is right. When you spend time focusing on what's not right, what needs to be adjusted, changed, or fixed, you miss the opportunity to really see your child.

One of Oprah's favorite lessons comes from Nobel Prize–winning author Toni Morrison and the question she asks of all parents: When your child walks into the room, do your eyes light up?

"When my children used to walk in the room, when they were little, I looked at them to see if they had buckled their trousers or if their hair was combed or if their socks were up," she told Oprah in 2000. "You think your affection and your deep love is on display because you're caring for them. It's not. When they see you, they see the critical face. But if you let your face speak what's in your heart . . . because when they walked in the room, I was glad to see them. It's just as small as that, you see."[14]

Do your eyes light up when your child walks into the room? Or are you focused on your own needs and agenda? Children want and need to be seen in the world. They want to be seen and heard for who they are.

When you really look at your children and see them for who they are, you validate their existence. We all have a common need for validation. We need to know we matter, and what better way to show your child that he or she is seen than by really seeing them in all of their goodness? See them less critically. Notice what they're doing right instead of what they've done wrong. When we focus on what is right, that becomes their focus too. Simply by acknowledging their act of being kind to their sister (when normally they aren't!) encourages them to be kind in the future. Telling your child "I really appreciate you cleaning up the kitchen when I was sick" helps them to feel good about themselves and increases the likelihood of them being helpful in the future. Remind yourself to focus on the good in your child. The next time your child walks into the room, I urge you to let your face light up with the love that you already have in your heart for them.

Journaling Exercises

- How would you describe the lens that you see your children through?

- Can you reflect upon a time when you were able to see your child with soft eyes?

- What did you notice about your child's behavior when your eyes became hardened?

- How did the different lenses help or hinder your relationship?

- How did you feel when you read the question, "When your child walks in the room, does your face light up?"

- How can you change your focus so that your eyes light up for your children?

Seeing Who They Really Are

When you look back at both personal and professional relationships, can you remember a time when you felt like an outsider, didn't quite fit in, or couldn't be you? Perhaps you felt the need to hide the real you in order to conform.

We've all been seen as someone we're not. This can happen on a daily basis as others make assumptions about us. There have been times in my life when people have assumed I was a snob or thought that I saw myself as superior to others. I explored this further and was told that this assumption was based on my quiet nature. Because I tended to be quiet in group situations, they quickly assumed that I was conceited. I was surprised to hear this. Assumptions are made in our world, often incorrectly, and people are unfairly judged with a broad brush. There is often fear beneath assumptions.

It is easy to be misguided in your assumptions, especially with your children. Because you're their parent, you may assume you know them best. Maybe; maybe not. Although you may think you know them and may be right on the mark sometimes, children are complex beings. Also, how they are being at this moment may not be how they'll be in the future. I often remind parents that their children aren't "baked" yet. They are still developing, so who you see today may not be who you will see tomorrow. I often receive calls from mothers concerned about their child's lying, so much so that they wonder if the child is becoming a pathological liar. If you've had these concerns about your child, let me reassure you that all children lie and that it's usually in an attempt to avoid doing what they've been told to do or to avoid punishment for what they've done.

Just because your teenager lies about their research project and promises you they didn't know it was due yesterday doesn't mean they're irresponsible or lazy. What it may mean is that they were more concerned about not being invited to a party over the weekend (that everyone else was going to, or so they thought) that the research project was the last thing on their mind. Even if they have forgotten assignments in the past, there is usually more going on than pure laziness. They may need help with organization or time management, but assuming they're lazy—and leaving it at that—does not help them learn responsibility.

Again, by quickly making assumptions based on past experience, you may miss an opportunity to see your child in a different way. Your child has her own thoughts and voice. You can learn more about your child by allowing her to use her voice. It's easy to ignore what your child is trying to say (often through her behavior) because of your own need to teach, correct, or maintain your mom power, when, in fact, dropping your need to be in control offers you an opportunity to connect with your child, gain a better understanding, and honor their uniqueness.

One of the best ways to acknowledge your child is to first acknowledge their feelings. I once worked with Kate, a mother of a ten-year-old girl. Kate's daughter, Emily, was "very strong-willed," according to her mother. Kate was very frustrated with her daughter's need to have the last word. As much as Kate wanted to allow Emily to express her feelings, she noted that there never seem to be an end to Emily's frustration. She further explained that Emily liked to argue and did this most often with her mother. According to Kate, Emily and her mother argued several times each week when it was time to leave for Emily's ballet lessons.

Emily had begun taking ballet lessons when she was four. Initially, her lessons were once a week, but because of her ability, her instructor recommended that Emily attend three lessons per week. Kate was thrilled that Emily had been asked to join the more advanced students. Kate had practiced ballet as a child and was also very talented. She majored in dance in college and planned to join a professional ballet company but was not able to fulfill her dream due to a car accident. Despite Kate's own wish to become a professional ballerina, she believed her daughter was fulfilling her own dream.

From the time Emily could walk, she loved to dance, and although Emily was initially excited about going to lessons more often, it wasn't long before she began to protest going to ballet class. Each time Emily told her mother she didn't want to go to ballet, an argument would ensue. Emily ended up going begrudgingly but would be sullen in the car before and after the lesson. I suggested to Kate that perhaps her daughter didn't want to take ballet lessons anymore. Kate resisted my advice that she have a conversation with Emily and encourage her to voice her opinion about continuing ballet. Kate insisted that Emily wanted to take ballet lessons but was probably just going through a phase. "I think she'll come around," said Kate.

Kate stated that she too remembered sometimes not wanting to go to ballet class. Again I reminded Kate that it's important that children feel seen and heard. Kate reluctantly agreed to talk with Emily about her thoughts on ballet. The following week when I met with Kate, she told me that she was disappointed when she found out that Emily didn't want to continue ballet. Emily told her mother that although she enjoyed it when she was four, she now found it boring and hated going every week. She said that the only reason she liked to go was to see her friends. Emily told her mother that she continued to do this for her but that she wanted to play soccer instead.

Although Kate was disappointed and was tempted to guilt her daughter into taking more lessons, she didn't. Kate remembered when she was Emily's age and was forced to take piano lessons. Kate's mother was a concert pianist and envisioned her daughter following in her footsteps. Although Kate continued her piano lessons until she was seventeen, she resented her mother because of it. Similarly, ballet was Kate's passion—but not her daughter's.

Kate later told me that she learned an important lesson by allowing her child to have her own voice and honoring her wishes. Simply by encouraging Emily to have her own voice, Kate honored her daughter for who she was, not for who she wanted her to be.

Your children have a voice. It's important to allow them to use it. When you're able to honor who they are (not who you want them to be), you allow them to grow into who they were meant to be. When you're quick to see your children for who you think they are, not for who they truly are, you miss out and so do they. Open your eyes and really see them—perfectly as they are, beneath all their behavior and defenses. This is their true essence.

Who You Are as a Parent—Seen through the Eyes of Your Child

If you were to see yourself as a parent, through your child's eyes, would you parent any differently? I believe that we all might be more mindful of our parenting if we were to examine how we appear in the eyes of our children.

When you reflect upon your childhood, how did you see your own parents? For a moment, I'd like to take you on a journey back to your own childhood. When you think about your childhood, do you have memories of warm, loving feelings and experiences? Or was your experience different?

During workshops, I often ask parents to think of one word that captures the essence of their childhood. What word would you choose to capture the essence of your experience? My word is "uncertain."

I was raised in a family with an alcoholic father and a mother with borderline personality disorder. I was never quite sure how my day would go and was hyperalert to help keep the peace in the family. No one assigned me this job; still, I took it on with fervor, as children often do. Although my dad was a loving father and I was "Daddy's little girl," I could not depend on him to be there for me. Through my eyes, as a child, I learned to watch for signs of my mother's instability, which was ever-changing. To the outside world, she appeared caring and kind, and she was, at times; but often, behind our closed family doors, she became someone else. I always sensed an unhappiness in her, which sometimes turned into anger. Through my lens, I watched and waited for the other shoe to drop and for her underlying anger to erupt.

As a result of my own uncertain childhood, I vowed I would be a perfect mother for my children and create a perfect childhood for them. I, of course, never wanted my children to suffer as I had. In doing so, I created other problems for my children and myself. I set us up for frustration because, in my best effort and attempts, I actually created unrealistic expectations for my children and myself.

Your childhood experiences leave lasting impressions—ones that you carry into your adult life. How you were parented often becomes a blueprint for the way you parent your children. You may consciously or unconsciously choose to parent precisely as you were parented, not knowing any differently. If you grew up in a dysfunctional family, as I did, you may choose to parent 180 degrees opposite of how you were parented. Either way, your children are watching. Just as you watched your parents and learned from them, your children are watching and learning from you. They are learning how to be in relationships, manage their emotions, and fit into their world.

Your children watch you intently. Have you ever noticed that your child imitates your actions and words? This was brought to my husband's attention when our son was four years old. They were out in the yard one afternoon, and our son happened to notice his dad's baseball cap was turned backwards. Without a word, our little boy walked around the corner of the house and returned with his baseball cap reversed. Not a word was said between the two, but it was evident that our son was emulating his dad. For my husband, this became an important wake-up call to his responsibility as a father. He began to watch his own actions more carefully and was much more mindful of his language, as he consciously tried not to let curse words slip from his lips!

Children, both little and big, are watching. Their internal lenses help create their experience. Their childhood experiences leave an impact on them, both positive and negative. How your child sees and experiences you has the potential to either enhance or diminish their way of being in the world.

As an adult, their childhood experiences will influence how they interact with the world. Have you ever been in a relationship with a spouse, family member, or coworker whose behavior you began to anticipate based on your past experience? Were you able to relax and feel safe in their presence, or were you on edge because of what they might do or say? We carry memories with us and are often easily triggered by them.

Perhaps if we were all to pause as parents and take a look at ourselves through our child's eyes, we might choose to act differently. By no means does this mean that we conform to how our children want us to be or that we cater to their every whim. What this does mean is that you have the opportunity to consciously choose how you want to be remembered as a parent when one day your child is asked: "What one word captures the essence of your childhood?"

Journaling Exercises

- Do you remember watching your parents while growing up? Choose several memories and describe what you saw.

- How would you describe your mother? Your father?

- What one word describes the essence of your childhood?

- How do you think your child would describe you, their mother?

- What one word do you think your child would choose to describe their childhood?

- Imagine that the word you chose in the above exercise was actually the word that your child would choose. Would you be satisfied with their word, or would you like it to be something different? If you'd like their word to be different, explain why.

- What can you do to influence how your child views you as a parent?

꧑   If you made those changes, how might things change in your
relationship with your child?

Out with the Old, In with the New

Are you ready to see yourself and your child through clear eyes? To
be more curious and allow for the possibilities that your child holds?
You may have resisted doing this before, possibly from fear. But remember: the truth can be freeing. I'm not asking you to throw out
all your old assumptions and beliefs, but acknowledge them and
then carefully select what still fits. Perhaps you'll allow yourself to
admit that you're not the perfect mom (Who is?) and be courageous
enough to come clean and say that motherhood is not all fun and joy.
When you let go of judgment or your need to see things as you want
them to be, you can then look at motherhood truthfully. You're able
to discern what is still true and what you need to let go of. You're
given the opportunity to reframe situations and view them from a
different perspective.

Your perception of yourself and your children ought not be
constant but flexible. Flexibility allows you to let go of your firmly
held perceptions. Byron Katie, in her book *Loving What Is*, teaches
us to question our assumptions and beliefs. She states, "I discovered
that when I believed my thoughts, I suffered, but that when I didn't
believe them, I didn't suffer, and that this is true for every human
being. Freedom is as simple as that. I found that suffering is optional. I found a joy within me that has never disappeared, not for a
single moment."[15]

When you're able to let go of long-held beliefs and see things as
they are, you discover a freedom that allows you to create new visions
of your child, yourself, and motherhood—and to simply embrace and
celebrate the messiness of being human.

Journaling Exercises

- ✆ Are there realities that have been difficult to for you to look at, for yourself and your child? If so, why?

- ✆ Choose two different situations that you would like to see with a clear, soft lens (to reframe the way you've been looking at a situation).

- ✆ What changes could you make within yourself to help support the new reality in each situation?

- ✆ Knowing what I know now, I intend to . . .

Chapter 4

The Messages We Send Our Children—They Share Them with the World

Shame, blame, disrespect, betrayal, and the withholding of affection damage the roots from which love grows. Love can only survive these injuries if they are acknowledged, healed, and rare.

—Brené Brown, *The Gifts of Imperfection*

*m*any years ago, I received an important message from my mother—one I've never forgotten. One winter afternoon, my mother hosted a girlfriend gathering. My brothers and I played quietly in the next room. The women were a close-knit group, but what brought them together was their shared experience of motherhood. The mothers looked forward to gathering each month. Children were not included, which left the moms free to share their stories, joys, and frustrations. They benefited from the social interaction, and their time together became a support group. The only children present were those of the mother hosting the gathering.

The mood was light as the mothers chatted about their busy lives. After a while, my mother invited my two brothers and me to join the grown-ups for juice and cookies. We were excited to join the party! My older brothers and I not only were enjoying our cookies but felt special being included with the grown-ups. We sat on the floor at our mother's feet, wanting to be close to her. But then, at one point, we heard her say to the other mothers, "Well, I did the best I could with what I had to work with"—as she pointed to us, her three children sitting at her feet. She laughed as she spoke, but looking back, I believe her laughter seemed to be more of a nervous giggle. The room became silent as the mothers looked down at their dessert plates, unsure where to look. Those words—*I did the best I could with what I had to work with*—were spoken by my mother. I remember that my brothers and I sat there, looking at each other and then looking at her. Maybe we had heard wrong; maybe we had misunderstood what she meant. Surely she wasn't talking about the three small, well-behaved children sitting quietly by her feet?

That was not the first or last time my mother spoke those exact same words. It seemed to become her mantra, especially when she gathered with friends. Those words stayed with me. They haunted me. They motivated me to try to be the perfect daughter (as if I wasn't already good enough). Years later, those words reminded me to never to speak about my children in this way—and they inspired me to do the work I'm now doing.

I later discovered my mother was suffering from borderline personality disorder, which helped to explain her erratic behavior. However, those words spoken by my mother many years ago stayed with my brothers and me on a deep, emotional heart level. I sometimes wonder if those words entered our DNA. I know they cut us to the quick. We internalized her words and carried them into our adult lives. Her words created a message of unworthiness. I'll never know if they were spoken intentionally or unconsciously, but it really doesn't matter, because they were spoken. Spoken words can never be erased.

Over many years, with a lot of self-work, I have learned to reframe those words—to look at them differently. I am now able to say: "Yes, my mother did the best she could with what *she* had to work with," as in herself with her limited capability and skills, the broken part of herself that still harbored and acted out her own childhood wounds. Those words, uttered by my mother, were a result of and influenced by the damaging messages she received as a child.

Chapter Summary

Language matters. Most likely you still remember hurtful words spoken by your parent, grandparent, neighbor, or teacher. Those words may have been spoken with good intentions or not. It doesn't matter. What does matter is how you choose to speak to your child— and you have a choice each and every day.

Beyond the words we choose, children also receive unspoken messages throughout childhood. The first and most important messages come from their parents. Most children internalize these early messages and carry them, consciously and unconsciously, into adulthood. Not all messages are negative or hurtful. Children carry negative messages, but they also carry the positive ones they receive. All of these messages have the power to shape how children see themselves and how they relate to others.

Messages Matter

Undoubtedly you have an assemblage of messages you've held onto from childhood. Hopefully, more are positive than not. Recently, I spoke with my sister-in-law about her childhood messages. She was gifted with these messages and holds the first two dearly.

- Enjoy the little things and sweet moments . . . they may not come again.
- You are special because you are Irish.
- Careful; you are getting too big for your britches.
- Wake up with a song.
- Don't believe everything you hear.
- Men will not buy the cow if they can get the milk free.
- You have a brain—use it.

Hopefully, you're able to recall some of the more positive messages from your childhood—ones that you may be passing onto your own kids. You might be playing negative messages over and over again in your mind. There's a chance you've tried to forget or block out the negative ones. Some messages, too painful to recall, may be suppressed—buried deep within. It's not until someone or something triggers you that some hidden messages begin to resurface.

As a parent, you have an opportunity, for you and your child, to change your story by rewriting these messages. You have the ability to clarify and alter the messages that you've carried for years. To rewrite history for yourself, your children, and your family. As a result, you can move forward and work to create healthy messages. Family messages, passed from generation to generation, can be rewritten in such a way that they will have the power to transform and heal generations to come!

Does this sound impossible to you? It's not. But before this can happen, it's important to identify and unravel the many messages that you've been sent in one form or another. You may not have received some of these messages from your own family, but nonetheless, you received them throughout your formative years. Messages that have stayed with you, that have left you feeling *not good enough, less than—* messages of *shame*. These messages have more than likely dragged you down and hindered your growth. You might also be inadvertently sharing these same messages with your own child.

Messages from childhood are sent not just by parents but by siblings, too. Even the most loving siblings can hurl a hurtful message when frustrated or jealous. Any child is capable of name-calling. They may make fun of one another, especially when a parent isn't present. After all, siblings compete with each other and vie for their parent's attention. I remind parents that even their best-behaved child is capable of sending hurtful messages. Besides modeling healthy communication within the family, it's important to keep an ear out for what's being said between siblings—those messages matter, too.

It's essential to take a look at the messages you received as a child, to examine what was communicated to you. Take some time now to reflect on your own childhood messages. The time spent will benefit not only your growth but also your child's.

Journaling Exercises

- What messages, both positive and negative, did you receive as a child?

- Which ones have you carried from your childhood?

- What messages have served you?

- What messages have hindered your own growth and happiness?

Mixed Messages We Send Our Children

We all have the ability to send mixed messages to our children. Here are some mixed messages, created by Nicole Schwarz, mom, parent coach and family therapist, and founder of Imperfect Families. She states, "No parent is perfect. No child is perfect. No family will have crystal-clear communication 100 percent of the time. Life happens. People feel stressed. They misunderstand each other. It's normal. Communication is a work in progress." We've all probably been guilty of sending confusing messages at some point.

This can happen when we say one thing but actually mean something else entirely.

- "You can ask me anything . . . but not right now."
- "You can tell me anything anytime . . . just not that."
- "Hands are not for hitting . . . except when I spank you."
- "It's not okay to yell . . . unless it's me yelling at you."[16]

Even at a young age, kids are wise to hypocrisy or double standards. Parents should lead by example. Think about whether you've ever said something similar to the following:

- "You're always playing that video game." "Just a minute, I'm on my phone."
- "Always tell the truth." "Let's just say you're still three so you can get in free."
- "It's okay to make mistakes." "You spilled the milk again!"
- "You don't have to be perfect." "A 'B' on your test? What happened?"
- "I love you no matter what." "Go away; I'm so frustrated with you."
- "I know you two can work it out." "That's it—you're both grounded."

☸ "Whatever you're feeling is fine." "Settle down and stop being so angry."[17]

These messages create confusion, but they can also teach our children to feel ashamed of themselves. Shame distorts a child's perspective and damages their sense of self. According to Brené Brown, "Shame is the intensely painful feeling or experience of believing that we are flawed and therefore unworthy of love and belonging." She goes onto say that "shame is universal and one of the most primitive human emotions that we experience . . . to feel shame is to be human."[18] We all experience shame. Shame drives our way of being and causes us to say or do things. It also influences how we relate to others. Unexamined, shame can create the blueprint and set the groundwork for how we show up in the world. Shame, if left to its own devices, can become the reckless driver of our lives. It can prompt us to harbor feelings of unworthiness. It can also create behaviors that we're not even aware of.

According to Brown's research, "Shame needs three things to grow out of control in our lives: secrecy, silence, and judgment."[19] As children, many of us were taught to hide our shame. Speaking of shame was neither welcome nor encouraged. Most of us were never encouraged to question our messages of shame, nor did we learn how to rid ourselves of shameful messages—and so our shame grew. When shame is allowed to come out into the open and we're able to talk about it, it loses its power over us.

However, it's our own underlying feelings of unworthiness, when left unaware, that we project onto others. We all have the power to shame others, just as we've been shamed. All we have to do is turn to the media to see the rampant shaming of others. We also have the opportunity and responsibility to stop the shame and blame that has become widespread in our society—and it begins in our own home. The very way you treat your children teaches them how to treat themselves and others. It is our obligation as parents to stop the shaming and blaming of children. Shefali Tsabary, PhD, author of *The*

Conscious Parent, states, "Self-esteem, which is born of feeling loved, worthy, listened to, and connected, is the driving force of good behavior—not fear of punishment. Shaming to make a kid who already feels bad feel even worse is nothing short of a recipe for disaster."[20]

As parents, we unconsciously shame our children in an attempt to make them behave—to conform to our wishes. It occurs most often when we're overwhelmed or frustrated. We experienced shame when our parents also used this same tactic. You may have heard some of these statements as a child; you may have even found yourself using these same words with your own child:

- What is the matter with you? How could you be so stupid?
- What were you thinking?
- How many times do I have to tell you?
- Why can't you be more like your sister?
- I'll give you something to cry about!
- You're acting like a spoiled brat!
- Stop crying—only babies cry!
- You should have known better!
- Just go away—leave me alone!
- You're so sensitive!

Language matters and has the capability to build a child up or break them down.

> While [humiliation] may solve the initial problem, the long-term consequences can be incredibly damaging. There is ample evidence from academic research that shows that when parents consistently use shame or humiliation as a punishment, children grow up to be more depressed, anxious, and less confident than children who aren't subjected to such discipline.
>
> —*Gary Walters, PhD*

Children can be shamed without their parent ever speaking a hurtful word. According to Peter S. Silin, MSW, RSW, and author of the article, "Shame: The Emotion That Runs Us and Ruins Relationships":

> The development of shame often happens through the attachment and separation process between children and parents/caregivers occurring at a very young age. When the relationship with parents or caregivers is difficult or ambiguous, shame can result. It can also occur through trauma, when a child feels abandoned or has been sexually abused. In their world, the only way they can make sense of what has happened is to blame themselves. For example, if a parent goes away, the child may think they did something wrong. If a parent is angry, the child may think it is his fault.[21]

Whether words are spoken or unspoken, children pick up on our energy and body language. They are very intuitive and also apt to create stories of unworthiness, especially if messages are ambiguous. Be clear with your messages. Choose your actions and your words carefully. Next time you're running on fumes, having a bad day at work, or feeling completely overwhelmed, remind yourself that words are very powerful. Once spoken, they cannot be retracted. Before you speak, take a moment and breathe. Remind yourself that your words matter. Before you speak, ask yourself these questions:

- Is it necessary?
- Is it true?
- Is it kind?

Shame is the most disturbing experience that a child can ever have about themselves; no other emotion feels more deeply disturbing because in the moment of shame the self feels wounded.

—Gershen Kaufman, PhD

Journaling Exercises

- Before reading this section, what was your understanding of shame?

- Had you ever thought about how your own shame is easily triggered by your child, especially when they push your buttons? Whatever your child does to triggers your shame, it is likely these shame triggers occur in other areas of your life. For example, if you feel your child disrespects you, there are probably others in your life that disrespect or minimize you. Can you identify triggers that are also common in other areas of your life?

- Have you found yourself saying the same shame messages to your child, repeating your parents' words?

It's often thought that shame and guilt are the same, and they are often used interchangeably. Take a moment to consider the difference. According to *Merriam-Webster*, guilt is "responsibility for a crime or for doing something bad or wrong" or "a bad feeling caused by knowing or thinking that you have done something bad or wrong."[22] A child feels guilty because his or her actions have affected another. For example, a little boy runs through the house, knocks over his dad's favorite coffee mug, and experiences feelings of guilt. Shame, however, says, "I am not good enough; I am not lovable; I am not okay." Guilt often precedes shame. A child who feels that their *actions* were "bad" may tell themselves that *they* are "bad." The same little boy who knocked over his dad's favorite coffee mug feels shame if he's repeatedly been told that he is "bad" when he does something wrong. If his parents perpetuate this message, the child will continue to judge his own actions and worthiness as "good" or "bad."

Negative Messages We Send—Even with the Best Intentions

Even the most well-meaning parent makes mistakes at times. Most parents know the detrimental effects of telling a child they're stupid or bad. Many parenting books instruct parents to comment on the child's behavior rather than their character. Most parents understand the importance of saying "You made a bad decision" rather than "You are a bad girl." Besides the more obvious communication faux pas, some mistakes in communication are not as obvious. Ron Taffel, PhD, author of the article, "Parenting Style: The Negative Messages That Even Good Parents Send," discusses destructive comments that parents make.[23] Here are some that might resonate with you.

- After finding out your child has been excluded from a friend's birthday party and in an attempt to make them feel better, you may say, "I know how you feel." But you really don't. You can imagine how they feel, but you don't really know. In your attempt to be supportive, you may actually upset your child even more. Assuming to know how your child feels often only fuels their fire and shuts down communication. It is helpful to empathize with what your child feels by saying, "You seem sad. Would you like to talk about it?" As a result, they feel heard and understood.

- Suppose your daughter comes home from a playdate in tears and says, "I don't ever want to play with Claire again!" You may be quick to respond, "Claire is a nice little girl. You don't really mean that." Maybe she does; maybe she doesn't. But by telling her that what she is saying is not true, you deny her feelings. You may feel justified in saying this because normally Claire is a nice little girl. Or maybe she's the daughter of your closest friend and you're trying to avoid an uncomfortable situation. Either way, your comment denies your daughter's feelings, which has the potential to make her doubt her own feelings in the future. When you allow your child to express their feelings, whatever they might be, they learn to trust them. When you encourage them to talk about what upset them, while providing guidance, they learn to understand and own their feelings. This also provides an opportunity to help your child learn to problem-solve.

ꙮ Sometimes we label our children. Labeling children limits their potential and can be destructive. Telling your child "You're the athlete in the family" or "You're our little dancer" may actually pigeonhole them. A particular label can also create pressure and make children feel they have to live up to a parent's expectation. Labels can limit the potential of other children in the family who may feel they can't attempt or measure up to their sibling's assigned role. You might discourage your child from seeing themselves any other way. When you encourage your child while acknowledging their efforts, you allow them to explore possibilities without being boxed in by a label. Praise them by acknowledging the beauty of their drawing rather than telling them they're the artist of the family.

ꙮ What about when we lie to our children? We might not even realize we're doing it. Ten-year-old Chloe walked into the room just as her dad stormed out. She looked at her mom and asked, "What's wrong?" to which her mother replied, "Nothing is wrong. Everything is fine." Clearly, it wasn't. But in an effort to spare Chloe the pain of her parent's heated argument, the mother lied. We've all done it at one time or another, and usually kids see right through to the truth. Or if not the truth, their imagined version of it. You're better off telling some truth. Chloe's mother could reassure her by saying, "You heard Dad and I fighting. We're both upset right now, but it doesn't have anything to do with you. You've done nothing wrong. This is between Dad and me, and we'll work to figure it out and make things better."

❧ Has your child ever come to you in tears after someone told them they were stupid or had crazy hair? Or perhaps you remember being told mean-spirited things by your classmates. It doesn't feel good and is especially hard to hear as a mom. After all, our job is to protect our kids, right? But sometimes we inadvertently add to their hurt when we respond, "I love you just as you are. You are perfect!" If your child is aware his hair is frizzy and out of control, telling him he's perfect does not negate his frizzy hair. A child who clearly knows that they're in the lowest reading group and struggles is very aware of their situation. If you first acknowledge their feelings and ask them if there is anything you can do to help them, they might be open to exploring their options. Maybe a new haircut or hair product is in order. Perhaps hiring a reading tutor to help boost their reading skills might give them the confidence they need and help improve their ability to read. You can't always protect your child, but you can help them explore their feelings and empower them to make changes in their life.

Do any of these sound familiar? Most likely, if some of these words have escaped your lips, you were simply trying to make your child feel better. Or perhaps you were frustrated, overwhelmed, or feeling powerless. Don't beat yourself up—we've all been there. Yet you have the opportunity and challenge to not go there again. It takes courage to self-reflect and examine the messages you've sent to your child. It also takes time. Invaluable time that I urge you to use now, today, to take a closer look at the messages you're sending your child. Are they healthy or filled with underlying words of shame that may impede your child's emotional development? It's impossible to make healthy changes if you're unaware of what needs to change.

Journaling Exercises

✎   What are some messages that you've been sending your child
       and would like to change?

✎   Can you identify any triggers that influenced the words you
       used with your child?

✎   Choose two negative or mixed messages that you think your
       child received from something you said. (No self-judgment!)
       Alter the two messages to create more positive ones. State them
       more clearly and see if you can add a positive spin to them.

The Impact of Shaming

I don't want to spend too much time discussing the impact of negative messages that we send to our children, but I know the detrimental
effect it can have on children. It is imperative to be able to recognize
the signs and understand the long-lasting effects. It is only with these
tools that we can understand where and how we must change our
communication.

Emotional shaming is abusive. It can occur in any family. We don't
want to believe that we could shame our children, but it's often done
unconsciously. When our own acceptance of our children is dependent on their behavior, our love becomes conditional. In our attempt
to get them to conform to how we think they should be, we exert control. But what gives us the right as parents to control our children or
their behavior? It's often in our attempt to control them that we resort
to shame. It may not be intentional, but the end result is the same.
Shaming disables kids. It stops them in their tracks. The effects of
shaming are often silent, making us unaware unless our eyes are open
to the signs.

A child who is berated for spilling their milk and looks down or
away from their parent experiences shame. A child who retreats to

their room after being told they are a disappointment experiences shame. A little boy who is yelled at for asking his mother a question and stands in silence as tears stream down his cheeks experiences shame. A little girl whose mother has posted a YouTube video of her daughter throwing a temper tantrum has experienced shame—publicly. Private shaming has the same effect as public shaming, because it takes only one person to witness and feel the shame: the child.

Shaming can often occur when a parent feels frustrated, angry, or powerless. The parent resorts to shaming because they've lost their way. They make the assumption that it's not only their job but their right to control their child. In their attempt to raise a well-behaved child, they end up creating a child who lacks confidence in himself and his decisions, a child who grows up and views the world through eyes of unworthiness. Messages of shame stick like glue and stay with the child for many years—often into their adult life. Children internalize these as messages of unworthiness. They believe that without the approval of others, they are unlovable. Are we to believe that our child's self-worth should be dependent upon our approval or disapproval of them? I hope not. Yet it is through our daily interaction with children and the messages we send that we influence their own feelings of self-worth.

Karyl McBride, PhD, LMFT, and author of *Will I Ever Be Good Enough?*, offers this: "When children are emotionally or psychologically abused, they grow up feeling unloved, unwanted, and fearful. Normal development is interrupted, and it sends the wounded child into exile. This is when negative internal messages are developed and why we have so many adults today feeling 'not good enough.'"[24] This is not the legacy we want to offer our children as they leave the nest.

In *The Gifts of Imperfection*, Brené Brown discusses how we defend ourselves from shame. She notes, according to research by Kate Horney, that we either move away, toward, or against shame. Those that move away from shame do so by silencing themselves, withdrawing, or keeping secrets. Those who move toward shame seek to keep the peace or please others, at their own expense. Behaviors of those who move against shame are aggressive in nature, are controlling, and can act out by shaming others. Brown concludes that "shame is about fear, blame, and disconnection."[25] Shame has the ability to perpetuate shame. Those who have been shamed continue to carry shame, and its effects touch everyone, in one way or another. It's not until we uncover the roots of our shame that we are able to heal and rewrite our stories.

It is my belief that parents have the power to end the shaming of kids. Language matters, and once aware, you have a choice each and every day to choose your words carefully. Your messages have the ability to either create a sense of worthiness in your child or make him feel unlovable.

Journaling Exercises

☙   Can you recognize any similarity in the shame messages you received as a child to the ones you're sending your child?

It takes courage to examine the words and messages you are sending to your child. Are there messages that might be shaming your children, either consciously or unconsciously? We've all done this—we're human. It takes a brave and courageous mom to honestly admit that she has shamed her own child. Even the most loving parents have unconsciously shamed their child.

Be brave . . . be bold . . . and be willing to see the error of your ways. Your child will appreciate it, and their growth depends on it. What messages would you like to change?

Children Carry Their Messages Out into the World

Children take their feelings of self-worth, or lack thereof, wherever they go. This is most obvious in the child who bullies. Their lack of self-worth and feelings of not being good enough motivate them to belittle others, all in an attempt to make themselves feel *better than*. Some children who bully have been bullied at home or have witnessed their parents bullying others. And lack of parental guidance and discipline can contribute to bullying when there is no moral sense of discerning right from wrong. Other children lash out because they are impulsive and have difficulty controlling their emotions and aggressive behavior. Children who struggle in school either academically or socially may feel the need to be better or stronger than a vulnerable child in their class—which can lead to bullying.

There are many reasons a child bullies. However, it's important to note that even the best of parents may have a child who bullies. Whether receiving messages inside or outside the home, the messages of being *less than* have been planted, messages that can create an unconscious need to fit in or feel *better than*.

Adults who have been shamed as a child exhibit their shame in many ways—some you may recognize in yourself or others:

- Feeling vulnerable and fearful of exposing themselves to the world
- Feeling unworthy and never good enough
- Believing they can't be one who makes a difference
- Feeling *better than* or exhibiting grandiose or self-centered tendencies
- Becoming defensive when given feedback, often perceived as criticism
- Quickly blaming others in fear of being blamed themselves
- Apologizing incessantly and assuming that their actions must

have contributed to the problem; assuming responsibility for
the behavior of others

- Feeling like an outsider; having a pervasive sense of loneliness
even in the presence of others
- Projecting onto others characteristics that they do not like
about themselves
- Believing that they must do things perfectly or shouldn't try
at all
- Blocking their feelings, which can result in compulsive
behavior such as workaholism, shopping, substance abuse,
eating disorders, gambling, or list-making
- Having little to no emotional boundaries and often feeling
violated by others
- Developing relationships with others based on dependency or
codependency[26]

Toxically shamed people tend to become more
and more stagnant as life goes on. They live
in a guarded, secretive, and defensive way.
They try to be more than human (perfect
and controlling) or less than human (losing
interest in life or stagnated in some addictive
behavior).

—*John Bradshaw,* Healing the Shame that Binds You

Shame is pervasive. Brené Brown refers to shame as a "silent epidemic." She states:

It's a problem of epidemic proportions because it has an impact on all of us. What makes it "silent" is our inability or unwillingness to talk openly about shame and explore the ways

in which it affects our individual lives, our families, our communities and society. Our silence has actually forced shame underground, where it now permeates our personal and public lives in destructive and insidious ways.[27]

Until recently, shame was never discussed. Shame research provides valuable information to stop this cycle of shame, because when we *know better*, we can *do better*. This is not to blame or shame you but to wake you up as a mother. To inspire you to reflect on your own messages from childhood. To be aware of your own emotional patterns and wounds. It is said that the teacher teaches what they need to learn—I am still learning. I hope you are too. Your child's overall emotional and physical health depends on it. It is through your willingness and courage that you can begin to break the cycle of shame. To be conscious of the messages you send to your child so that they will be gifted with many healthy messages to take out into the world.

Positive Messages Help Grow Healthy Children

Positive messages that empower children and boost their self-worth are like wildflower seeds planted in a meadow; they blossom and spread over time. Sometimes, it's the smallest of seeds or messages that garner the most vibrant flower. A child who is told that they are loved for who they are (without any qualifiers) is given permission to grow into their perfect self.

Two longtime coaches conducted a survey of college athletes, which lasted over several decades. The athletes were asked, "What is your worst memory from playing youth and high school sports?" Their overwhelming response was "The ride home from games with my parents." They referred to their parents' comments about their game, their performance—and how the child could have performed better. Chances are they already knew they could have done better; they didn't need to hear it from their parents. However, the message that brought them a lot of joy (and I believe probably improved their performance) was "I love to watch you play." Simple as that. This simple yet powerful message has stayed with many college athletes. Messages have the power to build or destroy. Watch your child light up when you simply say, "I love to watch you . . . color, dance, sing, jump." By simply witnessing and acknowledging how they're being in the world, you're allowing them to be themselves.

Rachel Stafford Macy, mom blogger and creator of *Hands Free Mama*, realized the power of her own words, words that help build confidence in her daughters rather than knock the wind from beneath their sails. The words "I appreciate you . . . I'm listening . . . You matter" are food for her daughters' souls. Saying to her children "Mistakes mean you're learning" and "You wanted it to be just right, didn't you?" allows them to make their own choices and to feel what they're feeling.

Rachel offers this to remind us of the power of our words:

> Like sunlight and water to a plant, these words nourish the deepest parts of the human heart and foster growth in all areas of life. Hence, I call them soul-building words.[28]

Your messages have the power to nurture your child's heart and cultivate their growth. Your beliefs about your child also have the power to influence your child's self-beliefs. Most likely, you're able to recall healthy messages that you received as a child. Some of them you may have passed onto your child.

The following are examples of healthy messages that all children would benefit from receiving:

- I love sitting next to you!
- When I look at you, I smile.
- I love watching you wake up in the morning.
- I love watching you sleep.
- I can see you have been working very hard.
- I notice that you like to take your time to think about

something before you make a decision—take as much time as you need.

- 🐾 Today was a tough day, but we did okay, and we'll try again tomorrow.
- 🐾 You must be proud of yourself.
- 🐾 When you were at school today, I missed you!
- 🐾 You handled that very well.
- 🐾 I could use your help with a project . . . you are so creative.
- 🐾 I love being your mom.

Positive messages you give to your children should not be dependent upon their emotions, beliefs, or behavior. There are no conditions. You appreciate them simply for who they are.

- 🐾 Knowing what I know now, I intend to . . .

Chapter 5

What Are We Teaching Our Children?

Whenever I held my newborn baby in my arms, I used to think that what I said and did to him could have an influence not only on him but on all whom he met, not only for a day or a month or a year, but for all of eternity—a very challenging and exciting thought for a mother.

—Rose Kennedy

*F*or all of eternity? That's a tall order, but, yes, through your daily interactions and teachings, you are the first one to influence your child. Do you think of yourself as a teacher? You *are* your child's first and I believe best teacher. Do you find this challenging and exciting as Rose Kennedy did, or does this terrify and unnerve you? Some moms vividly remember looking into their newborn's eyes and feeling an overwhelming responsibility, not only for their safety and daily care but also for ensuring they teach their child everything she needs to know before she ventures out into the world.

Chapter Summary

This chapter presents what I believe is the most effective way to teach children: by fostering a deep connection with your child. This vital connection is the key ingredient for imparting parental knowledge and improving children's behavior within and without the family. Children who do not feel connected to their parents become more resistant to parental guidance and rules. They may be compliant, but without a healthy relationship with a parent, their compliance may be out of fear of a parent's threat or fear of not receiving their parent's love. Other children rebel when they do not feel their parent's love.

This chapter goes beyond teaching behavioral strategies, something on which many parenting books focus. Instead, it encourages you to focus on yourself and your relationship with your child. You will find that a healthy connection with your child will help to create and reinforce positive behaviors far more than any short-term behavior modification strategy ever will. As you discover what your parenting style and experience has been, you'll learn ways to foster a healthy, open connection with your children, a loving connection that will serve you and your children for many years to come.

Becoming the Parent You Wish You'd Had

A few years ago, I made a conscious decision to shift the focus of my work and private practice. I now mostly work with parents, although I occasionally see their children. My previous work with children always included time with their parents, because I'm able to help children best by also helping their parents. I teach the teacher, so to speak. I believe children have the capacity to learn best from their parents. Along the way, I realized that rather than helping parents undo their child's learned behavior—or "mis"behavior, in the eyes of their parent—I could best serve families by instructing parents on how to teach their child important life lessons. As I shifted the focus of my practice from kids to parents, I began to notice that parents were still focusing most of their attention and energy on their children's behavior rather than their child's overall gifts, be it the child's sense of kindness or playfulness. Parents were so caught up in trying to fix their child's behavior that they lost sight of the bigger picture—their child and the importance of their relationship with their child.

Parents consulted with me looking for the perfect behavioral strategy to help "fix" their child's behavior. Although the strategies were effective and positive changes occurred, the behavioral strategies often became the focus between the parent and child. Sadly, the relationship was forgotten, or at least put on the back burner. When I mentioned this to parents, their response often contained a similar theme: *My relationship with my child will improve when their behavior does, and when that occurs, I'll naturally want to spend more time with them.*

I would propose that the opposite is true. Actually, I've witnessed this over and over with many families: when your relationship with your child improves, so does their behavior. Throughout my many years of experience working with parents and kids, I can assure you that *it all begins with the relationship.* The most effective way to teach kids is through your relationship with them. The key ingredient for imparting your parental wisdom and improving your child's behavior is having a healthy connection with them. Children who do not feel connected with their parents are more resistant to parental guidance and rules. They may be compliant, but without a healthy, connected relationship, their compliance is likely out of fear. This fear might be of a parent's threat of some sort of punishment or fear of not receiving their parent's love. Other children may choose to rebel.

Can you think of anyone who was overly compliant or rebellious in your family of origin? Maybe you learned at an early age that being compliant was in your own best interest. Your parent may have even referred to your as their "easy" child. Perhaps you were told you were such a good girl who never bucked the family system. Maybe you were the peacemaker in your family and behaved accordingly, in an attempt to not upset anyone. Or you might have been the one to rebel against your parents, especially if you had an authoritarian type of parent to whom compliance was expected. The rigidity in your family may have been more than you could tolerate. So, in an effort to be seen and heard and not be controlled, you fought back.

Not all overly compliant or rebellious children are disconnected from their parents. However, when rebellion or overcompliance become ingrained behaviors as a result of disconnection, they become the child's default mode. The stage is set. Behavioral patterns begin to develop and are reinforced by both parent and child.

In order to determine how you can best teach your child, it's important to reflect on how you, as a child, were taught. How did your parents teach you? Take some time to view your childhood retrospectively. Can you remember some of your most memorable lessons? How did you learn them? Did you learn from your parents' constant lectures? Probably not. If your parents were the type who nagged, did you find yourself tuning them out after a while (like the parents in the Charlie Brown cartoons)? Maybe you had parents who shouted orders at you but rarely engaged in two-sided conversations where you actually felt heard. Or maybe you had parents whose teachings were left unspoken, after which you were left to wonder what you were supposed to learn from the experience. Perhaps your parents weren't taught how to express their emotions, so they lacked the skills to teach you. No matter what type of parents you had, and no matter how well meaning, you may discover now how you could have benefited then if your parents had taught you in a different way. By identifying the pros and cons of your own childhood lessons, you'll likely be better able to consciously choose how you want to be as your own child's teacher. Your teaching style will be closely related to your parenting style.

Since the advent of the "super baby" movement (over the last two decades), which purported the importance of such things as baby flashcards and early introduction to foreign language, even more pressure has been placed on parents. Many parents have felt compelled to enroll their babies and toddlers in early enrichment classes, fearing they would fall behind other children. Recently, during one of my parent workshops, a group of moms compared schedules with each other about the number of activities their children were involved in. Many of these activities revolved around classes, either academic, musical, artistic, or related to sports. These scheduled activities seemed to take up most of the children's afternoon and early evening. A couple of moms even expressed concern that if they didn't start their child in soccer by age four, their child would never be able to play soccer in school because the competition was too great. You, too, may have succumbed to this fear, as many moms do. Please listen—I promise you that your child is going to turn out just fine whether you sign your child up immediately or wait another year. This common fear among parents perpetuates more fear. Be the courageous mom who does not give into fear. I can tell you that I have seen many children and teens in my practice who were overwhelmed, anxious, or burnt out from their many scheduled activities. All they wanted to do was quit and stay home! Some even told me that they begged their parents not to enroll them in the first place.

Before you begin to explore how or what you should teach your child, I want you to hear this: you will have many opportunities throughout your child's life to teach them, and you will have many chances to get it right. Because of our obsession to be good mothers—to be the best mother to our child—there are times when anxiety may override our capacity to see what we're doing exceptionally well, alright, or the best we can in the moment. Remind yourself that although your daily interactions with your child may not be perfect, you're doing the best you can in that moment. Ruminating on everything you think you've done wrong will only erode your joy and self-confidence. And your child will benefit by having a confident mother and teacher, one who can teach with confidence while being able to assess and alter "lesson plans" and actions as needed. One who is striving to do better but not wasting energy on trying to obtain perfection. A mom who understands what may have worked with her child yesterday may not work today or next week.

The specific methods you use to teach your kids will change; your personal style, the structure you provide, and your ability to follow through with consistency (more often than not) will help create a stable foundation for all the learning in your home. Children are ever developing and open to learning. It's a matter of discerning how your child learns best. One child may learn best visually, whereas another child might be an auditory learner. You may even have a child that struggles with learning but picks up the teaching quickly once they're able to get their hands involved. The kinesthetic child is a "hands on" learner. Digging their hands into the playdough, goop, or sand might provide the perfect learning experience for them. Children as well as adults have different learning styles. If you have more than one child, you've probably already discovered that their learning styles are very different, as are their temperaments.

Although most parents know the basic lessons to teach children—including learning the alphabet, manners, and right from wrong—parents lose sight of the bigger picture. I'm talking about the important life lessons that will help serve your child as they go out into the world. Lessons that will help set them up for success throughout their life. How and what you teach will set the foundation for all of their learning.

Your Parenting Style

There are as many different personality types as there are parenting styles. In the 1970s, Diane Baumrind, PhD, studied interactions in the home between parents and children. She developed a theory which identified four different types of parenting styles. She concluded that the way children function socially, emotionally, and cognitively was dependent upon their mother and father's styles of parenting.[29]

Most parents resonate with one style over another. As you review each parenting style, try to identify the one most similar to your style of parenting.

Authoritarian Parenting

- Rigid and rule driven; children are expected to follow the rules
- Fear-based punishment is often used as discipline
- Children aren't given choices (as a result, they don't learn consequences from the choices they make)
- A common refrain: "Do it because I said so—I'm the parent!"

Permissive Parenting (Indulgent)

- Very little structure or limit-setting; day-to-day life can often be chaotic
- Parents are lenient for fear they'll anger their child
- Parents often want to be their child's friend
- There is little discipline

Uninvolved Parenting (Permissive)

- Parents often lack parenting skills and knowledge
- Little to no rules or limit-setting

- Parents are often unaware of child's behavior or whereabouts
- Out of neglect, children often end up raising themselves

Authoritative Parenting

- There are rules, but exceptions to the rules are permitted at times
- Consequences are used rather than disciplining in a punitive manner
- Positive consequences are available (praise, rewards, etc.)
- Limits are set, but the child is taken into consideration (their feelings, temperament, etc.)

Many parents possess different aspects of the various parenting styles. Although your primary style of parenting may be permissive, occasionally your child may try to wear you down, begging you for "just one more cookie." At that moment, you're pushed to the limit, triggered, and bam—you're the authoritarian. Out of frustration and desperation, you yell, "No more cookies—you know the rules!" All in an attempt to let them know who's really in charge! On the other hand, as an authoritative parent, you're willing to be flexible in an effort to strike a compromise with your teen. Although teens are apt to push the envelope and want to bend the rules, sometimes it's perfectly acceptable to do so; your teen's curfew might be 11:30 p.m., but you're willing to extend it until 12:30 a.m. for a special date night. Some parents feel the need to hold fast to their rules in order to make sure their teen doesn't "win" or take advantage of them. Actually, listening to your teen's point of view and your willingness to be flexible reassures them that they are seen and heard. Your willingness to bend the rules occasionally also helps your teen understand that sometimes you just need to say no.

Rarely do you find authoritative parents slipping into permissiveness—it's not in their nature. However, they may receive a wake-up call and have the opportunity to change the way they parent.

I worked with a mom whose primary parenting style was authoritative. On most days, she set limits, provided positive reinforcement, and occasionally bent the rules—until recently. She'd returned to grad school and was inundated with papers and projects. Her normal routine and energy level was compromised by her added responsibilities. Most days, she described herself as barely keeping her head above water—simply trying to get through each day with the kids. Although she was not happy with her overloaded schedule or present state of mind, she was merely trying to get through the semester. She admitted that when she was tired, which was often, she didn't have the energy to maintain the limits she had previously set for her kids. They easily wore her down, and she found herself giving in to their demands. She began to notice a change in her kids' behavior. They became more argumentative and seemed to have a sense of entitlement. The mom realized that even though she had the best intention to provide structure, guidance, and consequences for her kids, she was simply too tired. Naturally, it didn't take her kids long to figure out how easy it was to wear mom down. This mom, who previously parented in an authoritative manner, had slipped into permissive tendencies.

Each parenting style can affect a child in a positive or negative way. Children growing up with authoritarian-type parents are at risk for becoming rebellious. They are angry and resist their parents' attempts to control them. Because they are not given opportunities to make their own decisions, solve their own problems, and learn from experience, they often have low self-esteem. A defiant teen was brought into my office a week after an episode of alcohol poisoning. After meeting with the parents, it was apparent that their style of parenting was authoritative—"It's my way or the highway!" They held their teen tightly and controlled most areas of his life. This teen, now seventeen years old, had been severely restricted his entire life. Although he was compliant, due to fear of his parents, once he got out of the house (they reluctantly allowed him to get his driver's license), he went wild.

Fear is often at the root of authoritarian and permissive parenting.

Authoritarian parents fear loss of control. Permissive parents often fear the loss of their child's love. "If I say no, will my child still love me?" Parental fear and anxiety do not provide sound building blocks for raising healthy children. A foundation built on love and connection—which also includes discipline—is what your child needs and is asking for you to provide. Children of permissive and uninvolved parents typically have behavioral issues and often resist rules and authority. They struggle academically and tend to suffer from low self-esteem. They may also experience feelings of sadness.

Children of authoritative parents are raised in an environment that encourages the child to make their own decisions and problem-solve. These children have the best chance to be happy and successful in life. They are comfortable expressing themselves and usually learn to become responsible young adults. When a child feels loved and connected to their parents, they are more open to their parents' teaching.

During my first session with parents, I ask them to reflect on what they learned from their own parents. Parents who felt connected with their parents remember learning many life lessons—how to treat animals, the importance of kindness, or the value of honesty. Whereas those who felt less connected remember learning how to do various tasks—washing dishes, yard work, or doing the laundry. Think about how your parents taught you best. Did you learn from the parent whom you felt most connected to or the one who frequently lectured but paid little attention to you or your needs? Trying to teach your child skills and values without a connected relationship as the basic foundation is really only surface-based teaching.

I once worked with a father, Eric, who took his parenting role very seriously. Eric recounted many times when his strict father—who considered himself to be the "boss" of the family—threatened, "Do it now, because I said so!" Although he remembered what his dad taught him (how to tie his tie, cut the grass, and balance his checkbook), Eric was unable to remember much time spent with his dad. He stated that his dad provided for his family but was not the kind of dad who loved spending time with his kids. He was either working or watching TV. Even when Eric asked his dad to play football, his dad seemed to have more important things to do—like cut the grass. Eric longed for his dad's attention. He recalled his frequent attempts to please his dad, to "get it right," but never felt a close connection with him. Eric told me he felt his dad had trained him to make his own way in the world, but Eric realized even in telling me about his father that mostly what he learned from him was to try to be perfect. He feared the loss of his father's love and attention if he fell short of his father's expectations. His fears were associated with trying to please his father and make him proud.

As an adult, Eric continued to feel disconnected from his dad. Eric knew he wanted a stronger bond with his children than he had had with his own father. He wanted to teach his children, but first he wanted to deepen his connection with them. Eric realized this would take time. There wasn't a quick fix or a behavioral strategy to apply. Yet he realized this effort and his commitment would benefit him and his children immensely.

Your ability to connect with your child as a unique individual is directly affected by your parents' ability to connect with you during your childhood. Were you seen for who you were rather than who your parent wanted you to be? The way you were parented created opportunities for either connection or disconnection.

Pam Leo, author of *Connection Parenting: Parenting Through Connection Rather than Coercion, Through Love Instead of Fear*, references Theodore Roosevelt's quote: "People don't care how much you know until they know how much you care."[30] Children learn best when they know you care about them—when you see and connect with them as unique individuals.

Journaling Exercises

🕉 Based on your reading of the various parenting styles, how
     would you describe your mother's style? Your father's? If

someone other than parents raised you, identify their type of parenting style.

❧   What effect did their parenting style have on you, both positive and negative? Which parenting style do you feel may have better nurtured your growth (emotionally, physically, and intellectually)?

❧   What is your adult relationship like with your parents?

❧   Identify and describe your own parenting style. Do you feel this style best fits the one you wished your parents had had?

❧   Is your style of parenting the best fit for your children?

❧   Would you like to alter your parenting style? If so, to what other style?

❧   What would you have to do in order to change to a different style of parenting?

❧   Is there anything preventing you from making these changes? If so, what?

Breaking the Parenting Mold

Most parents express wanting to feel a deeper connection with their children. The depth of connection and the way parents connect with their children has shifted over time. Many parents of generations past held the belief that "a child should be seen and not heard." The focus wasn't so much on the connection with the child but the management of the child. Our current parenting paradigm encourages children to be individuals who should be seen and heard. John Becker, a marriage and family therapist, states that "the very philosophy of parenting has changed in the past twenty-five years." He further explains that although parents want to encourage "character and moral development" as much as past generations, we're going about it differently.[31]

Traditionally, parents focused on raising "non-self-centered, obedient children," whereas today, parents are more concerned with enhancing their child's "autonomy, self-esteem, and individuality."[32] The old parenting paradigm viewed the parent as superior to the child. This type of parent-child relationship assumed that the parent knew all, or at least better than the child. You may have experienced this pattern in your family of origin. This parent-child hierarchical relationship may seem normal and comfortable to you. The problem with this paradigm is that it encourages parents to attempt to control their child rather than connect with them. Parents from past generations viewed a child's lateness to the dinner table as a sign of disrespect and expected children to eat what was in front of them.

Some children nowadays often refuse to eat what's on their plate and expect their parent to make another meal for them—and today's parents often do. Overindulging your child does not serve their growth (or connection), but allowing them a voice does. The "conscious parenting" movement is a newer phenomenon in parenting. It encourages parents to be more mindful and awake in their parenting. Conscious parenting also asks parents to shift the way they see their children—not as an extension or smaller version of themselves but as a unique individual.

When you parent, it's crucial you realize you aren't raising a "mini me," but a spirit throbbing with its own signature. For this reason, it's important to separate who you are from who each of your children is. Children aren't ours to possess or own in any way. When we know this in the depths of our soul, we tailor our raising of them to their needs, rather than molding them to fit our needs.

—*Dr. Shefali Tsabary*, The Conscious Parent

Your child is a unique individual. Your ability to see them as such will help strengthen your connection. Your child is also much more apt to feel connected with you when they feel accepted by you—no matter how they're acting. Your ability to be present while acknowledging their presence, emotions, and unique way of being helps foster connection with your child.

As parents have become more mindful of their beliefs and actions, they've learned to become more attentive in their everyday lives. Rather than waiting until their child acts out and then trying to control their behavior in a punitive manner (reactive parenting), they become more proactive. They learn to think ahead and be mindful about the choices they make. Conscious parenting enables you to respond to your child in a calm, confident manner rather than to react in an irrational manner. This way of parenting first begins with connection—with yourself and your child.

How might your parenting role change if you altered your position? What if instead of being the superior trying to control them, you guided your child with yourself right alongside them?

Shefali Tsabary states, "If you want to enter into a state of pure connection with your child, you can achieve this by setting aside any sense of superiority."[33] Power comes from your ego, your "self," but not your true self. When we try to parent from our ego, which we all do, we inevitably try to take control. We believe our way is the right way. We become more reactive and less responsive to our child's needs. If you use a behavioral strategy that requires your child to stop a particular behavior by the count of three (a popular strategy used by many parents), you're using your power to control your child's behavior. Although counting to three often encourages a child to stop misbehaving, what lesson are they really learning? For some children, they learn to stop right before they hear the number three. Is this type of parenting effective? In the short term, perhaps, but what about in the long run? The use of counting to control behavior is reminiscent of Captain Von Trapp's attempts to control his children in *The Sound of Music*. By blowing his whistle, he trained his children to stand at attention. They learned to obey, but it was at the cost of their relationship with him.

Love is the first step in developing a connection with your child, but it isn't enough. It also requires time spent, intentionally created just for you and your child—time that is honored and revered. Love between a mother and her child begins before the child enters the mother's life. The bond between mother and child is natural and vital to the child's emotional development. Love and connection deepen as the child grows. Many years ago, a slower lifestyle supported this connection. Extended families were often readily available to support the mother so she could nurture her infant, thus strengthening the bond. There was less separation between parent and child.

In our current society, mothers often return to work within weeks, extended families aren't nearby, and life's demands are that much greater. A child's need for connection hasn't changed, but our lives have. There are more demands and distractions than ever before. It takes more of a conscious effort and commitment to create and sustain this important bond between parent and child.

> At every level and every stage of development, there is either love—and with it, growth—or fear—and with it, protection and a thwarting of growth.
>
> —*Bruce Lipton*

You may already feel connected to your child because you spend a lot of time with them. I'd ask if your time is spent like most parents, running from place to place, struggling with your kids to do their homework, or reminding them over and over to take a bath. If this is how your time is spent, you're not alone. Parents report spending a lot of time with their children yet have begun to realize the time spent with their children in this way is not relationship-building. The to-do list becomes the focus of the relationship.

A lot of mothers tell me that even when they're not physically with their children, they're thinking about or worrying about them. Our society has become increasingly child centered, yet I would propose that children feel less connected with their parents, in spite of their time together. I've certainly seen this in my own practice. It's not because of lack of love or interest in their children but more a result of parents' demanding schedules, digital device distraction, and a workload, both personally and professionally, that hinders connection.

I recently coached a mother about her relationship with her daughter. They were experiencing what I consider the usual ups and downs that occur during the teen years, but the downs had far outweighed the ups over the past year. A short while after we began working together, the mother resigned from a job that made many demands and kept her long hours. While working from home for a few months before beginning a new job, she began to notice a dramatic difference in her daughter's mood and behavior. The daughter wasn't as reactive and appeared less stressed. The mom began to observe her own mood and behavior and realized she could say the same about herself. We discussed how stress can have a negative effect on the whole family system. Your presence matters and is fundamental to building and nurturing connection.

Kids of very loving parents complain that they don't feel close to their parents. Young children wish their parents had more time to just play. Other children have expressed that they love going on family vacation but wish that the vacation included only their family, not the family friends. I've worked with many teens who also wish their parents would spend more time with them. Parents of teens are often shocked when I tell them this. Most teens won't ask for more time with their parents and act disinterested when pressed to spend more time together, yet teens long for this. I'm hesitant when I share this information with parents (with the child or teen's permission) because most parents are already overwhelmed or guilt ridden about how little time they spend with their child, one on one. Some parents become angry and defensive; they feel their whole life revolves around their child and wonder why their child would feel this way. I remind them that it's not about the amount of time but rather how the time is spent.

Parents of younger children seem to understand this because they're able to reflect on time spent with their children when they were able to be fully present and simply enjoy special moments together. But as their child becomes a tween or teen, some parents believe their presence is not as important as when their child was younger. This is reinforced by their teen's independence and overwhelming desire to socialize with their friends. However, it's the parent's presence and connection that enables a teen to deal with life's stressors in a healthy manner. Because teens are able to depend on their parent, to help guide them both emotionally and morally, they can learn to become emotionally independent adults. Teenagers need their parents more than ever during these formative years. The connection between a teen and their parent is vital to the teen's ability to navigate these tumultuous years. A sense of connection also directly affects a teen's decision-making and behavior. Research shows that teens who feel connected with their parents are less likely to engage in risk-taking behavior. Teens who eat dinner with their family five nights per week are much less likely to smoke cigarettes.

The love for your child along with your willingness and commitment to create healthy connections will offer the gift of a loving, deep relationship—a gift that is priceless for you and your children. It is because of this relationship that your children will be much more inclined to want to behave in a responsible way—for themselves.

Making the Connection

Your influence as a parent is either enhanced or diminished by the strength of your connection with your child. This connection is not solely about the time you spend with your child; it's also about attunement—your ability to be receptive and aware of your child and their needs. You become attuned to your child's needs from early infancy.

Even without their verbal cues ("I'm hungry," "I'm tired"), within a few weeks, you're able to pick up on their cues of hunger and fatigue. This is a skill that you'll learn to develop as they grow out of infancy. Have you ever been in a relationship where you didn't feel seen or heard? When you felt that the other person just didn't "get" you? Kids feel this too. Your ability to attune to your child allows them to feel valued and understood, both of which help them to become a healthy emotional being.

So what are the key ingredients for a healthy connection with your child? Pam Leo, author of *Connection Parenting*, explains that creating a connection with your child occurs by connecting:

- With yourself
- Through respect
- Through listening to your children's feelings
- Through filling their "love cup" (think of this as a "love bank account"—the more you fill this, the more love your child will feel)
- Through expression of love and loving acts
- Through communication
- Through decoding your child's behavior
- With your own needs[34]

A strong, healthy connection when your children are younger will help to sustain a connection during the teen years. As you learn to parent a teen differently than a young child, you also learn to connect differently. Respect for your child speaks volumes. They learn respect through watching you. Your children should not respect you out of fear or because you're the parent. You build connection with your child by listening to their feelings and dropping your need to know or be right. Remaining open and curious about your child's feelings—without feeling the need to fix—allows a child to feel and express their emotions. If you're unsure about what your child is feeling, ask them or mirror the emotion that they're experiencing. For example, think about a child who bursts into tears when their friend breaks their favorite toy. They are expressing emotions of sadness and anger. As a parent, rather than try to fix the situation, minimize it, or distract children from their feelings, give your child permission and space to feel and express their emotions, all the while letting them know that you are there for them—in a supportive and connected way.

Communication is essential to connection. How you speak to your child speaks volumes about how you relate and connect with them. When children are spoken to in a respectful manner, connections grow and children are more readily available to learn. They trust us and are more open to our influence. Maybe you were raised in a noisy family where you had to raise your voice to be heard. Or perhaps you came from a family in which a lot was communicated by silence. You may have learned when you missed your curfew that your parent's cold "silent treatment" was tantamount to their loud, angry outburst. Although it was a much quieter parenting technique, it screamed anger and disconnection. Children learn patterns of communication from their parents, both healthy and unhealthy. A mother who yells at her child every time he misbehaves communicates anger. A father who frequently shuts down emotionally when his child becomes upset may inadvertently communicate isolation and abandonment to the child. Alternatively, a parent's ability to have open and honest communication with their child not only models healthy communication for them but also helps to create a deeper connection.

Even if you feel very connected to your child with the strongest parent-child connection, you will not always understand what makes them tick. Chances are your kid's behavior confuses you or keeps you guessing. How on earth can you figure out or decode your child's behavior? Do you sometimes wish you could look inside their brain to see their thoughts? You might not find the answers you're looking for. When your child jumps on the dog, dumps an entire bag of sugar on the floor (in an attempt to "help" you cook), locks their younger brother in the closet, or eats a worm, and you ask them *Why?*, isn't their usual response *I don't know*? Believe them when they say this.

The truth is they often don't know. They've simply reacted without a single thought or plan. One way to explore your child's behavior, especially if you've noticed a recent change, is to take a look at your own behavior—have you been more stressed or frustrated? Has your family been on the run and forgotten to include some downtime in your busy schedule? Maybe you've noticed that your child's behavior worsens because of certain triggers—hunger, fatigue, or when transitioning from one activity to another. Whatever the reason for their behavior, when you remember to connect with them first, your child will be more apt to open up to you. Your reaction or response has the ability to deepen connection or create a disconnect.

The last important part about creating a connection is to connect with your own needs. We'll delve into this a bit more in Chapter 11. For now, know that if you're meeting others' needs without attending to your own, your connection will break down—with yourself and your child.

Teenagers

Before moving onto the next chapter, I'd like to include a sidebar about teenagers. Connecting and communicating with teens is a whole different story. Ethan Hawke, actor and father of four, sums it up best when he says, "Even though kids are hard to reach, it doesn't mean they don't want to be engaged."[35] Sometimes you have to be a bit more creative in your attempts to reach out and connect with your teen. But first, you need to drop your assumptions and be curious.

Parents have been forewarned about the difficult teenage years. So much so that some parents dread the day their kids become teens. Others view their teenagers as someone that will hopefully "outgrow this stage" sooner than later. Teens can be a lot of fun once you have a better understanding of them. They're not always easy to understand, because they're still trying to understand themselves. From a developmental perspective, teens are egocentric but not as narcissistic as some might think. They're just a bit distorted in their thinking. Tweens and teens ranging from ages eleven to sixteen believe that everyone is acutely aware of them, watching and judging their appearance and behavior. It's as if they're on stage and the world is watching—this is often referred to as the "imaginary audience."

Can you imagine the feelings this might evoke if you felt you were on display—every single day? This in itself explains the irrational thoughts and behavior of teens. If you're a mom of a teen, you know exactly what I'm talking about. The fifteen-year-old who's gone through three outfit changes before seven a.m. and is still in tears when she leaves for school—because she doesn't have a thing to wear! Or the sixteen-year-old who has to fix his hair one last time before almost missing the bus. Their appearance is so important to them because they feel it's also important to everyone else they come in contact with.

Another aspect of a teen's development that's essential to understand is their need to individuate. According to Rebecca Fraser-Thill, author and professor of developmental psychology, "Individuation refers to the process of forming a stable personality. As a person individuates, he gains a clearer sense of self that is separate from parents and others around him. . . . Individuation occurs throughout life, but it is an important part of the tween, teen, and young adulthood years."[36] It's during the teen's developmental stage of individuation that they separate from their parents. Many parents feel hurt or rejected as their teen pulls away (some teens do this more gracefully than others), but it is a vital step in becoming a well-adjusted young adult. This is the time to loosen the reins, stay connected, and allow your teen to make some decisions for themselves. I once heard a psychologist tell parents of teens, "You've just been fired as your teen's manager, and you better work really hard to be rehired as their consultant." As a mother of four former teens and with many hours of experience sitting with teens in my office, I assure you these words were well spoken.

So how can you connect and communicate with your teen? In small and simple ways. Parents often feel the need to plan a lavish day with their teen in an effort to gain their love and attention. It's really the little things that matter. It's okay to let your teen know that you're missing the time you used to spend together. Not in a guilt-inducing way, but with a casual approach—"Hey, I miss you—can we hang out together soon?" Drop your own agenda and lower your expectations. Offer suggestions, but let your teen take the lead. Many teens tell me that they really do want to spend time with their parents, but not all day! After all, a social life is a teen's priority. Taking your son or daughter out for breakfast or lunch before they meet up with their friend is a great way to connect. Engage your teen in planning a date together. A quick trip to the mall and a movie can be a great way to reconnect. Some teens and parents have fun while playing golf, hiking, or working at a soup kitchen together. The key is doing something together that you both enjoy. Otherwise, it becomes a dreaded commitment.

And don't forget to invite their friends over. Your kids will appreciate it, and you'll get a glimpse into their social world. Some teens love to cook or do projects around the house. And your teen would much prefer your company while they're raking the backyard leaves!

Also, don't forget to listen when your teen is ready to talk—that's even more important than talking. Teens have lots to share when we're quiet and willing to listen. Try to be available when they're ready to talk. That might be in the car, late at night, or while taking a late-night walk. Teens are much more apt to talk when they don't have to make eye contact. Empathize with what they're saying, but don't try to fix their problem (unless they ask for your advice).

I often suggest a shared journal. This allows moms and their kids to communicate their feelings and allows the other the time and space to process what they've read and learned. It often takes the emotional charge out of the conversation and allows communication to remain open. I suggested this to one mother I recently worked with. Both she and her thirteen-year-old daughter seemed to be at odds most days. By the time they fell into bed at night, they were both emotionally spent from their attempts to communicate. The mother loved the idea of the journal, and the daughter soon found it very useful. They shared their thoughts not only when they were upset but also on a daily basis. Some entries addressed a recent disagreement, whereas others were for simply wishing each other a good day or saying *I love you, even though I don't always tell you.* Teens do want you in their lives, in spite of what they may be showing you.

And one last thing—don't forget to say *Goodnight* and *I love you.* Your teen still needs to hear this and will appreciate it (although they'll probably never tell you so).

Building and nurturing the bond with your child does not happen once and then you're done—it's a lifelong process. Yes, even into their adult lives. We have an opportunity and a choice as to how we relate and respond to our children. We are all social beings and wired for connection. It's the moment-to-moment decisions we make that either bring us together or allow us to drift further apart. Just like the sailor who adjusts the sails, you too can learn to tack your own sail as a parent.

Journaling Exercises

- Take some time to reflect on your ability to connect with your parents and your child. Do you remember moments of connection with your parents? What were you doing or not doing? Describe how you felt during those times of connection.

- Did you find yourself longing for more connection with your mom or dad? If not, who did you feel most connected to in your family of origin? Why?

- How can you tell when you feel connected to another person? Describe what emotions come up for you, how you feel in your body.

☺   Do you find it easy or difficult to connect with others in your life?

☺   How do you connect with your children? If you have more than one, are some easier to connect with than others? If yes, why do you think this is so?

☺   When do you feel most connected with your children? When do you feel least connected?

☺   Identify ways that you try to connect with your children.

☺   Do you notice a difference in your child's behavior after you've spent time together?

☺   Have you ever asked your child how they feel when they're connected to someone or something (their pet, for example)?

☺   List ways you feel connected to your child. Consider other ways to connect with your child—engage your child in a conversation about connection (they want and need your connection and love imagining and creating ways to connect).

☺   Knowing what I know now, I intend to . . .

Chapter 6

Children Are Our Teachers

A child can teach an adult three things: to be happy for no reason, to always be busy with something, and to know how to demand with all his might that which he desires.

—Paulo Coelho

Children are so wise, yet we often discount them as our teachers. After all, aren't we supposed to be their teachers, not the other way around? What could they possibly teach us that we don't already know? After many years observing children, both personally and professionally, I believe they have a lot to teach us, if we're able to slow down, watch, and be open to their lessons. When we consciously take the time to observe our children and their way of being in the world, we learn many lessons. Children are able to teach us in a way no one else possibly could. The closeness of a parent-and-child relationship alone, along with the countless hours spent together, provide many opportunities for children and parents to touch each other, even if we rub each other the wrong way. However, it's during those times that we're given a chance to clarify where the "rub" or irritation is coming from. It's through your many interactions, during hours spent caring for them and nurturing your relationship, that you can learn and grow.

Chapter Summary

Children are able to teach us many lessons if we let them. Simply by learning to see your daily interactions with your children from their perspective, you'll learn to shift your own. This will enable you to look at your children's behavioral issues in a different light—not as a problem but as an opportunity for growth, both for your child and yourself. It takes courage to soften your heart and eyes and allow yourself to be taught from the one you feel you should be teaching.

In this chapter, I discuss many of the lessons that children teach us and some of the ones that they wish we'd learn. Ultimately, these lessons do boil down to three principles: learning to be present, to be flexible, and to remain open-hearted. Our discussion of the individual lessons will show you how to put those principles into action. In the process of learning *how to learn* from your children, you'll be given the opportunity to discover even more invaluable lessons and messages from your wise teachers!

The Many Lessons Children Provide

In his book *Wherever You Go, There You Are,* Jon Kabat-Zinn refers to children as our "live-in Zen masters."[37] A Zen master teaches students about enlightenment and about becoming more awake and aware in our daily living simply by living life in the moment. Isn't that what our children do on a daily basis? They wake us up to the present moment again and again when we pay attention.

Sometimes, they bring us into the present moment in their playful way, when they jump into our laps and wrap their soft, cuddly arms around us. Who can resist the sweet hug of a child? Other times, they wake us up in the moment by irritating us or pushing our buttons—buttons that sometimes I feel they themselves installed! However, those buttons are our own, for us to examine on an up-close and personal basis. And when we do, we are given the opportunity to grow.

Your children are not only growing but are providing you with opportunities to grow as well. Do they realize that they're doing this? Probably not. Are they judging you as you're growing yourself? I doubt it. However, when you are not learning and growing as a parent and individual, they will often call you out. Think of a time when your child reminded you of a promise that you had made or a consequence that you didn't follow through on. Those are teachings.

Children provide us many lessons in many different forms. When we are open to their teachings, our learnings become limitless!

Children are mini-mirrors that reflect our negative and positive qualities. You might have noticed how your child lovingly talks to their stuffed animals or dolls in the same way that you talk to them. You may have experienced those warm, fuzzy feelings as you watched your child help a friend in a caring, loving way.

Besides your positive traits, you're also given the opportunity to see your shadow side through your children. Do you remember ever hearing your child use one of your expressions that you were least proud of? A mother told me recently that her own judgmental nature, something that she was not proud of, was evident when she heard her child repeat her exact words, in her exact tone of voice: "I can't believe that mom is letting her little girl eat those greasy french fries! Doesn't she know any better?" or "Those parents are bad because they are letting their child [fill in the blank]."

Common negative qualities we exhibit may include jealousy, anger, resentment, or judgment. I've worked with many parents who are reminded daily of their own quick-to-anger reactions when they see the same reactions in their children—often, parents who are anxious see anxiety in their children before others do. The saying "It takes one to know one" explains that we often see in others what exists in ourselves, though we may not want to look at it.

It takes courage to look at our weaknesses, our negative traits, and examine them and be comfortable with the feelings that arise. However, once you're aware, you have a choice. You can decide if you want to act from your shadow side or not. So the next time your child shines a mirror on an aspect of yourself you'd rather not see, be grateful for the gift you've been given. Your child has been your teacher, and as the student, you have been given the opportunity to learn from them. You then are able to make conscious choices about how you want to be in the world, for both yourself and your child.

Your children provide learning opportunities when they push your buttons.

Our buttons reflect our Achilles heel. Last year, I taught a class about how to become a calm and connected parent. Emily, a single mother of three, described to the class how her eleven-year-old son, Jake, pushed her buttons. He was the oldest child and very independent. He and his mother seemed to be at odds almost daily about his homework. The more Emily pushed Jake to do it, the more he resisted. They seemed to be caught in a vicious cycle of late assignments, video games being taken away, more pushing by Emily, and more resistance by Jake. Emily was totally frustrated.

When the parents in the class suggested that Emily look at what was driving her to keep pressuring Jake to do his homework, even though the frustration and anger between them was increasing, she first said, "Because I'm the parent—it's my job." We encouraged her to look more deeply and reflect about why having her son complete his homework was so important to her. After a while, she realized that her own anxiety was driving her behavior. She said that she was anxious because "if he doesn't complete his homework on time, it reflects poorly on me as his mother." After Emily took a few deep breaths and calmed down, she reminded herself that it wasn't up to her but up to Jake to complete the assignments on time. With encouragement from the other parents in the class, Emily decided not to continually remind her son about his homework. Jake had repeatedly told her that he was aware of his assignments and would complete them on time.

The class met the following week, curious to find out how Emily did with her decision. With a smile, she announced that she had not reminded Jake and that he actually had followed through on his own and completed all of his projects on time. Jake told his mother that he knew the consequence for not completing the assignments would be a weekend without video games, so he chose to do the work on time.

Emily was given a gift by her son: she learned to trust his ability to follow through and to let him grow and experience the consequences of his own choices.

Challenges we see as problems are often opportunities for growth.

Have you ever survived a problem only to look back and see that something positive came out of your experience? You may not have seen the silver lining at the time, but from the rear-facing seat, you may have been grateful for the experience. As a parent, you've probably helped your child with many problems and perhaps even encouraged them to see the opportunity in trying to solve it. Children often remind us of this when we're faced with problems. Think back to a time when your child overheard you struggling with something and quickly suggested another way to look at the situation. Maybe you were frustrated by the weeds growing in your manicured garden while your child saw the beauty in the wildflowers.

Children may also force us to question our own reality, to look at life from a different lens. Are you a glass-half-empty or a glass-half-full kind of person? If you're a parent with a glass half empty and have a child whose glass is habitually half full, I challenge you to spend some time with them and see how full your glass becomes! Most kids I know who are carrying around full glasses are happy to share life's abundance with you. Their positive attitude is contagious and helps to shift your negative thoughts. And when problems do show up in your life, your children can help provide you with a new perspective. Even the problems that they seemed to have created offer opportunities for learning and growth, both for yourself and your child.

Children help us question our reality.

As adults, we easily get stuck in our own way of being, with our own preconceived thoughts and notions. We assume we know, but do we really? Has your child ever questioned something that you thought to be true? When you've allowed them to question and you've taken the time to examine your thoughts, what did you find? Were you convinced what you said was true, or was your child able to help you see your "truth" in a different light? Children are great at asking questions. When we allow them the freedom to do so, sometimes they give us a gift of freedom—from our own mind!

Were you allowed to question ideas and statements when you were growing up? Did your parents encourage you or try to squelch your inquisitive mind? The next time your child questions your ideas or reasoning, you would be wise to be curious and see what you just might learn.

They teach us to slow down and live in the moment.

How do you typically move through your day? Are you on the fast-track mode or a bit slower? You've probably figured out by now that your children march to the beat of their own drum, some a bit slower than others. If you're a fast mover like I am, it's not easy to slow down. I was reminded of this a few years ago when I was hurrying through the airport with my four-year-old granddaughter. We both agreed that the "people mover" conveyor belt would be fun. However, I also knew walking on it would get us to our destination faster.

I didn't realize that my granddaughter's agenda was different from mine. I quickly realized that her way of riding the conveyor belt was to stand in one spot and let it carry her slowly past her surroundings to our destination. I, on the other hand, was trying to hasten our steps so that we could arrive at our destination sooner. Each time I gently nudged her to take a few steps forward, she said to me, "That's okay, Gramma; I'm good. You can keep walking, but I'm okay. I'm fine." Yes, my four-year-old granddaughter taught me to slow down and simply live in the moment.

Watch your children as they play. Observe how they move from one moment to the next, often lost in their own world. You might enjoy just allowing yourself to be in the moment, observing the simple pleasures of life that pass you by during your busy days.

Children teach us what is really important in our life—what to hold onto and what to let go of.

Children usually live moment by moment. By allowing themselves to simply live in the moment, children typically do not attach themselves to thoughts or things. They transition from this moment to the next. However, when your child holds tight to a thought about how much they want a dog and their never-ending quest to get you to buy them one, you can see that it is something obviously important to them—something worth holding onto. On the other hand, they may decide to let go of their need to win an argument with a friend because they care about their friendship too much to allow their disagreement to get in the way.

I remember when our four children were younger and our lives were busy with schedules. Most days I felt like I was constantly saying, "Hurry up—let's go!" Sometimes, the more I told them to hurry up, the more slowly they seemed to move. During a reflective moment, I realized that because of my own desire to always be on time, I was creating a hurry-up atmosphere in our home. Certainly, my kids didn't seem to care if we were always on time. That was my issue, not theirs. So I began to examine my need to be on time and reexamined our busy schedules to see what I could let go of. As a result, we spent less time rushing to "do" and more time at home just to "be." I realized that when I let go of extra activities, especially during the summer, our time together as a family was more rewarding and I was no longer the timekeeper. We began to carve out more time for fun activities and memory-making adventures.

The value of my intentionally created slowdown was driven home when, recently, our family was together for our third daughter's wedding. I loved hearing our adult children's stories of our fun outings together to the candy store when they were younger. They reminisced about how they were allowed to pick out any candy as long as it didn't weigh more than a quarter pound. They laughed about how they used to try to get the most variety within the weight limit. As I listened to them, I realized that the memories of simple trips to the candy store, which I'm sure did not include a "Hurry up!," had stayed with them into adulthood.

As we watch them grow and transform, children teach us that nothing is forever.

As you watch your children grow from infancy to childhood and beyond, I'm sure you're reminded of how quickly time passes. Although you may feel some days that time's going at a snail's pace, especially during the tough times, you've discovered that time does pass quickly. The behavior or attitude that drove you crazy before is not an issue anymore. And frustration and upset that you held onto probably seems insignificant now. Children remind us of the truth that nothing lasts forever and that "this too shall pass," both the sweet and the not-so-sweet times.

A mother recently shared a story with me about her learning from her baby. Abbey was thrilled when she found out she was pregnant. She had longed to become a mother and looked forward to sharing the experience of motherhood with her husband. Abbey had an easy pregnancy until her seventh month, when she developed complications. Her daughter was delivered early and because of breathing problems was put on a ventilator. The doctors were unsure of the baby's prognosis and prepared Abbey and her husband for the worst. Their fear and pain were unimaginable, yet as they watched their daughter in the incubator, they reminded themselves that life had no guarantees and that they would embrace every moment they had with their infant. The moments grew into days, and after six weeks in the NICU, their daughter, Alexis, was allowed to go home with them. Abbey learned from the first days with her daughter to embrace and appreciate what was, knowing that it might not last forever.

When children hold grudges, it's not for long.

It doesn't take long to realize that children are *in* motion and emotion! We often question how they have so much energy. Maybe their little bodies and minds are not loaded down with the burdens and to-do lists that we adults carry around. Your kids may also be adept at letting their own emotions out without any filter to catch them. Temper tantrums are a great example of a child's ability to let loose with their own emotions! As parents, we're given the task of teaching our children to regulate their emotions, but we can also learn from them about allowing ourselves to express our own emotions in a healthy manner. As adults, we might tend to hold in our emotions, which may not serve us or those around us. Can you think of a time when you wanted to express how you were feeling but held back, perhaps fearing the repercussions if you spoke your truth?

Although your child might pout about something, it usually doesn't take long before it's forgotten. I've worked with many mothers of girls who become wrapped up in their daughters' disagreement with a girlfriend. Have you worried about a problem your daughter or son is having with a friend? As their mother, you might hold onto the conflict that left your daughter in tears long after the two kids have resolved their problem! As parents, we could all learn from our children to let go of any long-held grudges.

Children are typically accepting of others.

Every day that I'm with children, personally and professionally, I'm reminded that they are much less judgmental than adults. They often see the good in others and are quick to defend another child's actions, even the hurtful ones. They are especially good at forgiving. I often remind parents that a child's ability to forgive works in our favor. When you've made a mistake as a parent, rather than holding onto your feelings of guilt, apologize to your child and then appreciate the fact that they are gifted with the ability to let go and forgive. Each day is a new day and another chance, as a parent, to get it right!

A couple of years ago, I had the chance to learn about the importance of letting go, forgiveness, and giving second chances. A seven-year-old girl named Chloe was my teacher. During our first visit together in my office, she said, "My mom doesn't fit into my family." She expressed this in such a graphic way that I'll never forget it.

Chloe held a ball made of many magnetic puzzle pieces in her hand. When all the pieces were put in place, it turned the puzzle into a ball. She quickly assembled the ball, but she held one last piece in her hand. She showed it to me and said, "This is my mom, and the ball is my family. My mom just doesn't fit into my family." When I asked her why, she said that her mom never gave her second chances and didn't play with her. She explained that her father and brothers always gave her second chances and played with her when she asked. During our play therapy session, Chloe shared that when her mother was mad at her, which was often, although she assured her mother that she wouldn't make the same mistake again, her mother never gave her second chances. When I asked the little girl what she meant, she stated, "If my mom doesn't get mad right away but gives me a second chance, then I can try again."

After working with me for two sessions, Chloe's mother learned to respond to her child rather than react. They began to enjoy more time together and found time for play. The last time I saw Chloe, she again showed me the magnetic ball and had one piece left out. She said, "Do you remember when I first came to your office and told you that my mom didn't fit into our family?" I told her that I did remember her telling me this. Chloe looked at me, placed the remaining puzzle piece into the ball, and exclaimed, "Mommy now fits into our family, because she gives me second chances and plays with me!" Second chances, not holding grudges, and offering forgiveness are some of the best lessons our children can teach us.

Children show up as themselves.

Small children typically don't worry about reactions to their appearance. When you watch your child choose their outfit in the morning, are you tempted to re-dress them in clothes that match? One of the first ways children declare how they are showing up in the world is through their clothing. They don't have much control over anything else in their life, but if given the opportunity, they can make their own fashion statement! Children have a natural ability to show up as they are. We can all learn authenticity from our children. Perhaps the next time you're tempted to show up as you think others expect you to be, be as brave as your child and show up just as you are.

Children laugh freely.

Spend an afternoon at the pool or in the park with your children, and chances are you'll be laughing. Research suggests that children laugh many more times per day than adults. They are also more spontaneous. Your children don't spend hours planning how they're going to spend their time. When given time, their day seems to unfold spontaneously. Their playfulness and curiosity seem to guide their activities, and they're adept at quickly deciding how they want to spend their time. Your children are not bogged down with responsibilities and don't take life too seriously. Again, they're great reminders to lighten up and live life in a lighthearted way.

What Your Children Want You to Know

Parents often express that they just wish they knew what their child was thinking. Although you may not always want to know what your child is thinking, I'd like to share a few insights I've gained from my many years working with children.

This is my life, not yours.

Our default mode as parents is to quickly step in and solve our children's problems for them. We do this because we love them and want to help them. We also do this because we don't want them to make mistakes, especially mistakes we have made. We don't want our children to suffer. However, when we put our teaching role aside, we begin to notice how capable our children are.

For a moment, I'd like for you to think back to some of the life problems you have encountered. Did you learn by figuring things out on your own, or were your parents quick to solve your problems? If your parents were quick to fix your problems, were you happy that they jumped in or do you wish they had allowed you to determine the solution for yourself? If someone solved your problems for you, did you learn anything in the process?

Truth be told, we learn more about ourselves and life when we put on our big-girl pants and face challenges head on. We learn when we take responsibility for solving our problems and recognize how we've participated in creating the problem to begin with. We have this same opportunity and responsibility to our children. We've all, at times, helped our children too much. Although we try to be helpful because we love them, we're inadvertently sending the message *I don't believe you can handle this. You are not capable.*

Is this the message you want to send to your child? We can and should help them navigate problems—but from the sidelines. This begins when they're toddlers and continues as they grow. Knowing what they're developmentally capable of (which varies with each child) helps guide your ability to discern whether to support their efforts or do it for them. When we calm our own anxiety as parents and remind ourselves how capable our children are, we're able to provide them the space and opportunity to solve their own problems.

Be a part of my life, but not my whole life.

Just as we all want to live our own life, so do our children. Here's the bottom line: kids want us around, but not all the time. All kids need their own space in which to engage and create their own life, to develop their own friendships, and to participate in their own activities.

Kids want us to be present for their sporting events and recitals but don't want us to be right in the middle of it. They want us on the sidelines, cheering them on, but not jumping into the middle of the activity.

Our children also want to know that we have our own lives and that we are not experiencing life vicariously through them. Kids need to know that we are self-fulfilled individuals and don't need them to fulfill us.

Chill out!

Has your child or teen ever told you to chill out? Maybe your kids are little and haven't reached this stage yet, but our children often ask us to chill out, to be less upset, and to not blow things out of proportion. They're asking us to calm ourselves down. They're hoping we will be less reactive and stay calm in the moment, even when they can't!

> Emotional reactivity is a parent's worst enemy.
>
> —*Hal Runkel*, ScreamFree Parenting

Lighten up and play with me.

Remember playing as a child? Most adults have become serious, and the more serious we become, the less we play. Sometimes, we seem to view play as frivolous, unnecessary, or a waste of time. When we allow it in our lives, play provides us many gifts. We can watch children and learn how to play—they know how to do it best. And they learn through their play. Children learn about relationships through their social interaction with other children. They also learn the art of negotiation, especially when they want a turn playing with that special toy. As Jean Piaget stated, "Play is the work of children."

Play also provides us with enjoyment. It helps to lighten our mood, our spirit. It gives us a valuable reason to lighten up and enjoy life. One of the best benefits of playing with our children is that it is relationship-building. We can spend time with our kids without giving them directions or correcting their behavior. We might be tempted to do some "parenting" during play, but if we're able to drop our teaching role and show up as a playmate, the magic of a child's imaginative world appears. When you're able to become your child's playmate for a while, dropping your need to parent, you'll experience the benefits of play and your connection with your child will become that much richer.

One of the first homework assignments I give parents is to play with their children, no matter what concerns they may be having. When parents engage with their child on a playful level, they begin to see their child in a different—and better—light. Their child is in their natural element with nothing to prove. They just show up, as themselves, and let their own light shine.

Recently, I worked with a mother who felt overwhelmed by her daily family responsibilities. She wanted to connect with her daughter in ways other than making sure her daughter finished her homework, took her bath, etc. Play was not among her list of responsibilities. I talked with the mother about the importance of playing and spending special time with her daughter. The next time she saw me, the mom said that she had gone into her daughter's bedroom one morning and asked her little girl, "Will you play with me?" The look on her daughter's face, the mother said, was priceless. "She looked surprised and not quite sure what to do. But her look of surprise turned into a big smile, and she accepted my invitation." I love the way this mother became playful, even in her request to play with her daughter.

So many times when our children ask us to play with them, we find ourselves saying "In a minute" or "Later" because we're feeling pressured to complete tasks and responsibilities. Perhaps asking your child "Will you play with me?" can be the beginning of many playful times and conversations.

Be here—right now.

No matter how convinced we are of the importance of being present in the moment, it's never easy, especially when our minds are spinning out of control. Have you ever been so caught up in your thoughts that your child has yelled "Mom, Mom, Mom! Watch me!" five times before you heard them? Every parent has been there.

Children are not distracted or overwhelmed by to-do lists or adult responsibilities. They are able to just be there—now. What a gift! Adults can experience this too, but it doesn't come naturally anymore. Being present in the moment is a skill and a muscle parents need to develop—one that takes practice. There are many different ways to practice being in the moment—to be mindful. When you focus your mind on what you're doing, you're mindful. Brushing your teeth, taking a walk, eating a meal, looking at a sunset, and sitting in silence are all activities that allow you to be in the moment. If you become distracted by your thoughts while you're engaged in a mindful activity, that's normal. Just notice your distracting thought, pause, take a breath, and refocus your attention.

Be the best you . . . for me.

Our kids want us to know that our *words* mean nothing without corresponding behavior. If our words do not match our actions, our credibility is zip. Our kids are watching us with laser attention to see if they can trust us, trust us to show up as their parent—not only talking the talk but walking the walk. They want to know they can count on us. That we will follow through on what we say, even if that means enforcing a rule or consequence.

Several years ago, I was working with the parents in a family of five. Their family and work lives were very busy, and consistency was not their strength. The parents expressed frustration that their children never "follow through with anything we ask them to do." One day I met with their eight-year-old son. I asked Ben what he would change if he could change anything about his family. He stated without hesitation, "I wish my parents would follow through with consequences." He went on to say that although they sometimes warned of consequences if he didn't do as they asked, rarely did they actually enforce the consequences. Ben wanted his parents to hold him accountable for his behavior and to follow through with the consequences that they had set. Your children, too, want you to be the parent who loves them wholeheartedly and follows through with your word.

I'll respect you if you respect me.

Over the years, many parents have sat in my office and vented that their children did not respect them. Their kids even had the nerve to talk back! When this is clearly a chronic issue, I often ask the parents if they respect their child. My question is usually met with resistance to the idea of *mutual* respect. Ask yourself if you believe, as a parent, that respect goes only one way. Do you believe that, as a parent, you are under no obligation to show respect to your child? If you want your children and teens to respect you, you need to be someone who can be respected.

Some parents say that of course they respect their child—but the child doesn't see it. That raises the question: how can we make sure our children and our teens know we respect them?

- By listening to them fully without judgment
- By acknowledging their feelings even when we don't agree or completely understand
- By asking them to help us understand better
- By not always having to be right
- By admitting mistakes we've made
- By apologizing to our children when we haven't shown them respect

Listen and Learn

Children are great "homeschool" teachers when we allow ourselves to be open to their lessons. Every day, they give us opportunities to learn and grow. This requires our willingness to be vulnerable, to look at our "shadow." By being real, being vulnerable, and showing up as our true, "messy" selves without judgment, we give freedom both to our children and ourselves. Freedom for yourself and your child to show up as you are, freedom to make mistakes and learn from them, freedom to express your own opinion, freedom to feel what you're feeling—in other words, freedom to be a whole person! Freedoms that ultimately contribute to your child's ability to see and connect with you on a real level.

Hands-Free Mama

I look at you and see the damage done.

"That's me," I say when my not-so-desirable qualities surface in you.

I'm too impatient.
I'm too controlling.
I'm too worry wart.

I'm too independent
too head strong
too overreacting
too stubborn
too sensitive
too head-in-the-clouds.

And I am afraid I've passed it down to you.
I'm afraid it's beyond repair.

But then I see you hold a puppy
Take the lead
Write a story

Run with your hair flying
Create like an artist
Laugh with your mouth wide open
Protect your sister
Wipe another's tears
Come up with a plan

And I say, "That's me," and perhaps I am not a complete mess.
There's some good in there.
And you're picking up on that too
Along with your own unique strengths, talents, and gifts.

And for the first time, I feel hopeful
That my not-so-desirable qualities can soften over time
That my rough edges can smooth out with each passing day.

And maybe I'm more okay than I thought I was.
And maybe you'll be okay too.
And maybe you already are.

So today when I look at you, I will try to focus on what's more than okay
In both of us.

—"More Than Okay," Rachel Macy Stafford, author
of the blog Hands Free Mama

Journaling Exercises

- Have you ever considered your children your teachers? What were your thoughts when you first read the title of this chapter, "Children Are Our Teachers"?

- Describe a situation in which you were aware that your child was your teacher.

- Which positive or negative traits do you have that you see in your child or children?

- Do you find it easy or difficult to see your negative aspects as well as your positive?

- Does your child push any of your buttons? If so, what are they? What triggers you?

- Are those same buttons pushed in your other relationships? If so, describe the circumstances.

- What would you like to change about yourself in terms of how you show up in life? What would it take for you to begin to make these changes?

- Do you find it easy or difficult to let go of hard feelings and forgive? Identify a circumstance that you're having difficulty moving past. What is stopping you from letting go?

- List three ideas in the section "What Your Children Want You to Know" that resonated most with you.

- Describe the significance that each of the three ideas had for you.

- If you could choose two things that you'd like to change about yourself or how you react as a parent, what would they be?

- List three action steps toward making desired changes that you are willing to commit to over the next week.

- Knowing what I know now, I intend to . . .

Chapter 7

Whose Behavior Problem Is It Anyway?

The sign of great parenting is not the child's behavior. The sign of truly great parenting is the parent's behavior.

—Andy Smithson

*Y*our child's ability to manage their own emotional reactivity is dependent on how well you manage your own. When your child's emotions and behavior are out of control, how do you handle your own—or do you? Are you able to calm yourself before you interact with your child, or do you open your mouth before your brain kicks into gear? Emotions are contagious. And your actions trump your words. No matter what comes out of your mouth, the emotions behind your words make all the difference in how your child sees and hears you, in how they relate to you. The most effective way you can help your child calm down is first to calm yourself down. Even when you feel the need to discipline (teach), do it with empathy and in a state of calmness.

Chapter Summary

It takes a great deal of effort and courage to recognize when our children's behavior is a reflection of our own, partially because we often don't want to see it. But as we courageously take responsibility for ourselves and honor our children's responsibility for their own behavior, we remove the biggest behavioral problem: our own emotional reactivity. And as we learn to manage our own emotions, we can model healthy emotional practices for our children, giving them the tools to become emotionally capable individuals.

Reactive Parenting Creates Bigger Behavioral Problems

During a parent coaching session, I listened to Angie, a self-admittedly frustrated and worn-out mother. She described a litany of behavioral issues she was having with her six-year-old daughter. After a while, I stopped Angie and asked her to breathe. Her breathing had become quick and shallow with each detailing of the transgressions she believed her daughter had committed, from disobeying to disrespecting her. Angie slowed her breathing and wiped the tears from her eyes.

"Why is it so hard for me to get through the day with my daughter? If this is how she is at six, I dread seeing what's she's like as a teenager. I couldn't wait to be a mom, but I'm not enjoying my time with her."

Angie's frustrations were typical of many parents I've worked with. I remember also experiencing the same frustrations with my own kids. Angie told me that everything seemed to be a battle with her daughter—getting up and dressed for school in the morning, brushing her teeth, doing her homework, and going to bed. She also said, "Anytime I tell her no, she throws a fit." I asked Angie what she had done so far to improve her daughter's behavior. She said she'd tried everything she knew to control her daughter's resistant behavior and outbursts.

"Nothing has worked, and my daughter's behavior is getting worse."

I asked Angie, "Whose behavior problem is this?"

She answered, "My daughter's, but I'm responsible for my daughter and her behavior."

"Are you?"

I'd like to ask you the same. Is your child's behavior your responsibility or your child's? You may believe, as many parents do, that you're responsible for your child and their behavior. When parents adopt this belief, they work tirelessly to control their child's behavior, often while trying to make sense of their child's seemingly illogical behavior. We wonder why it matters if the sippy cup is blue or green—*and why are they having another meltdown?* In an effort to "fix" their kid's behavior (as many parents have asked me to do), they consult parenting books, experts, mommy blogs, friends, and family. I frequently remind parents that neither their child nor their behavior needs to be fixed; they're not broken. Kids are little humans and are sometimes cooperative and well behaved—and sometimes they aren't. Sometimes their behavior makes sense, but often it doesn't.

Here's the good news. You're not responsible for your child's behavior; you're only responsible for your own. Please inhale slowly and take this in—it's important. If you knew this to be true (that you were not responsible for your child's behavior, only your own), would it help you feel better or worse? Would this knowledge lessen or increase your anxiety? The concept of not taking responsibility for your child's behavior may be foreign to you. If you're still in doubt, please keep reading. Even if you've read many parenting books convincing you otherwise, I'd like to share what I have learned over the years, both as a professional and a mom. A colleague and mentor, Hal Runkel, author of *ScreamFree Parenting*, solidified this concept for me. As a certified ScreamFree leader, I now know what I've suspected for a while: the best gift you can give your child is focusing on yourself. Although this shift might be new for you, your willingness to do so will benefit your child and yourself in many ways, for many years to come.

Hal Runkel, founder of the ScreamFree Institute, states, "Parenting is not about children; it's about parents."[38] He further explains by saying, "The only way to retain a position of influence over our children is to regain a position of control over ourselves"—our emotions and behavior.[39] The title, *ScreamFree Parenting*, may lead some parents to believe this teaching is not for them. I've worked with many parents who are quick to defend their parenting style—because they don't yell. Or if they do yell, they believe that yelling is the only way to get their child to listen. A mother recently told me that she tells her daughter to get ready for bed five times before she actually listens, and by the fifth time, this mom is yelling. But no matter our parenting style, we all *scream* in various ways—yelling is just the most popular version. We also scream when we:

- emotionally shut down and disconnect from our kids;
- manipulate or try to control our kid's behavior;
- overfunction (helicopter parenting) or underfunction as a parent;
- give up or give into our kids (because they've worn us down).

When we're frustrated and overwhelmed by our kid's behavior, we *scream*. Runkel believes that our worst enemy as parents is "our own emotional reactivity." I believe our worst enemy in all of our relationships is our own emotional reactivity. The ScreamFree Institute mission is to calm the world one relationship at a time. Their trainings have taken the team around the world teaching ScreamFree principles to parents, spouses, leaders, teachers, and military members. Imagine how our world might be different if every individual focused on themselves and took responsibility for their own emotional reactivity—if we each created a pause before we reacted and learned to respond instead. When you create a pause before you act, you respond in a more rational manner. The limbic system in your brain—the one handling your emotions—begins to calm down. Your response comes from a more peaceful place that helps you think rationally.

When you're fired up and act quickly, you're much more apt to react irrationally. Sometimes our behavior is more irrational than our child's. And we're the adult, right? Our kneejerk reaction does not help our ability to parent in a rational manner. Parenting from a calmer state allows you to make better decisions for both you and your child. The message Hal Runkel shares with the world is *Peace begins with pause*. Yes, you can have a more peaceful relationship with your children, but the peace begins with you.

This concept offers parents an invitation to broaden their perspective and a make a shift in the way they've parented. *ScreamFree Parenting* teaches a different and, I believe, better way to more effectively approach a child's problematic behavior. Although you'll continue to observe your child's behavior and have the opportunity to understand what lies beneath, you'll learn to focus more on yourself. In the process, you'll learn how your thoughts and beliefs impact your actions. This knowledge alone will empower you to self-reflect and alter your part of the behavior-problem equation. Your willingness to do so will lead to long-lasting, positive changes in your family. Your children will also appreciate your ability to own what is yours rather than project it onto them.

It is amazing to see the external results of internal change, particularly when reactive parents choose to become responsive. I've worked with many parents who were self-proclaimed "yellers." Although this was not how they'd intended to parent their children, when frustrated, many resorted to yelling simply as a tool to get their kids to listen. I advise them that not only is yelling ineffective with little to no long-term benefit, it's also harmful to the relationship with their child. Children do not learn by being yelled at. They learn you're quick to anger and that they have a good chance of delaying doing what you've asked—until you yell. They also learn to yell or emotionally withdraw.

When working with reactive parents, the first assignment I give them is to stop yelling for a week. You can imagine the look on a parent's face when they first hear this. Their initial response is often, *Oh, great; now what am I supposed to do? Yelling is the only way I can get my kids to listen to me and behave!* Although most parents are doubtful about the no-yelling assignment, they usually agree to try it for a week. One hundred percent of the parents who've committed to this challenge and stopped yelling (for the most part) were excited to report how much this changed their child's behavior in only one week. Did their kids suddenly become perfect, compliant children? Of course not. But what did happen was that parents began to notice subtle changes in their kids when they themselves stopped yelling. The kids became less reactive and more cooperative. The kids were also less resistant to engage in a conversation with their parents. Maybe they no longer feared the conversation would turn into a heated argument. Both parents and kids reported feeling heard. The focus between the parent and child was no longer just the task at hand but their relationship. It was through connection that the kids became more cooperative.

Focusing on Yourself

Once I began teaching ScreamFree Parenting classes, I added another component to the parents' initial homework assignment. I asked them to begin to identify what triggered their yelling—and to begin to focus on that. In addition, they explored ways to pause and calm themselves down. What I began to notice in my parent coaching sessions were parents sitting in my office with smiles on their faces. When I asked how things were going, most parents answered, "Things are so much better!" The parents began to witness and understand the power of the *pause*. This pause did not guarantee better behavior on the child's part, but it certainly guaranteed better behavior on the parent's part. The simple act of pausing (which is not always easy) became the impetus for change, not only for the parents but also for their kids. The pause is what allowed parents time to self-reflect and choose how they wanted to behave. Their own emotions and emotional reactivity were no longer dependent upon their child's behavior. Consequently, parents learned to pause and monitor their own behavior—and so did their kids.

There are thousands of parenting books on the market (approximately 72,000 as I'm writing this book!). The majority of the books ask you to focus on your child's behavior. After all, it's their behavior that's driving you crazy, right? So it would make perfect sense to focus on what's wrong or "broken" and attempt to "fix it." Most likely, this has been how you've approached your child's behavioral issues. This has been the way most parents have attempted to improve their kid's behavior. It's the same thing their own parents did, and their parents. The problem is that the focus is on the child, not the parents. When parents focus on their children, they often see improvement in their behavior—but only for a short while, because it creates a temporary change. Focusing on your own behavior, rather than your child's, may seem counterintuitive. Haven't we been told as parents to focus on our kids? Hasn't our culture become child centered? One would certainly believe so based on the behavior of many parents. Parents tell me quite often that their kids seem to be running the house. The parents' sole focus seems to be on their kids. They drive them to activities and make sure they have everything they need, all the while trying to keep the peace to avoid a meltdown. Many parents complain that their whole life seems to be about their kids—and it is.

This child-centric phenomenon in families is recent. Until the past few decades, parents did not focus as much attention on the needs of children but expected children to fit with the family's needs. The overfocusing on kids has also led to overfocusing on their behavior and ways to make it better. The problem, again, has been that the focus is misplaced onto the child. The moment you focus solely on your child's behavior, you stop focusing on your own.

I've worked with many parents who've spent countless hours and energy focusing on their kid's behavior, hoping they learn to become responsible. However, they've unknowingly gone about it in the wrong way. Because parents actually assumed more responsibility for their child, they also took on the responsibility of their child's behavior. The message they inadvertently sent to their kids was *I don't believe you're capable of handling this; that's why you need me to help you.*

Picture the teen who forgets (or neglects) to study for a science exam. However, this isn't an ordinary exam; it's one to determine the teen's readiness to be placed into a class for gifted students. Because the student didn't study, they didn't do well on the exam. Instead of allowing the teen to experience the consequence of not studying, the parent wrote a note to the teacher saying *My son was sick the night before the exam and wasn't able to study. Please allow him to retake the exam.* The note was written in part to help calm the parent's anxiety. *If my son doesn't get into the gifted class, chances are he won't get into the Ivy League college all of the men in our family have attended.* So the parent wrote the letter. What did the teen learn as a result? That mom or dad will save them and that it's okay to lie. (This actually happened. This same teen is now in college—not Ivy League—and struggling to keep up with the school's demands.) Helping your child learn to become responsible for their own behavior will serve them not only as they grow but also into adulthood.

Runkel states, "We are responsible *to* our kids, not responsible *for.*" He continues, "I am responsible *to* my child for how I behave, regardless of how he or she behaves."[40] This concept of responsible *to* rather than *for* is a game changer, once parents adopt this belief. If we assume responsibility *for* our children, we feel responsible for their behavior, their grades, the decisions they make, the mistakes they make—the list goes on and on. To calm our own parental anxiety, we not only assume this responsibility but also take on the responsibility of ensuring that they do everything right. Our belief as parents that *we know what's best for our children* creates our underlying need to control our kids—to make sure they don't mess up. Especially if we believe that how our kids turn out is ultimately a reflection of our parenting ability. This model of parenting only serves to increase and reinforce a parent's anxiety.

Once you begin to focus solely on yourself, you're given the opportunity to examine why you're quick to react. In the previous chapter, you began to look at your triggers, triggers you developed as a result of your unresolved childhood emotions. We are also triggered by our own parental anxiety. Our parenting becomes fear based. We play the incessant *what if* recording in our minds, often unconsciously. *What if* they don't study for the exam, or even possibly fail the exam? *What if* they don't make the football or tennis team? *What if* they miss the bus or misbehave in school? And why do we do this? If we believe that we are responsible *for* our children, then it's easy to also believe we're responsible for everything about them. The underlying belief becomes that our parenting ability is dependent on the safety and success of our children. After all, isn't our child's performance reflective of how they were parented? This may be what you believe, as many parents do, but is it true? If this is what you believe, then chances are you're working overtime to make sure your child doesn't fail at anything.

However, this very fear creates an unhealthy relationship with our kids. Our relationship then becomes conditional. Because of our underlying fear that our children will fail, we don't allow them to do so. We don't give them the opportunity to learn from their mistakes or failures. We also don't want our children to suffer. Very few parents allow their children to suffer, but sometimes suffering is just a part of life. It teaches children how to make better choices or accept what they cannot change.

I worked with a twelve-year-old girl, Amanda, who had been diagnosed with anxiety. I vividly remember my first visit with her when she
said, "I think you should really be meeting with my mom—she's the
one that's anxious!" This young woman was very perceptive.

When I'd met with her mother for the initial visit, she told me that
although Amanda had been a bit of a worrier when she was little, it
never was a big problem. According to her mom, Amanda was not a
big risk-taker and was bit slower to join the other kids in preschool
activities, but she seemed to do fine. In kindergarten, she was shy
but seemed to enjoy school. By second grade, Mom noticed that her
daughter began to worry about her school assignments. Mom shared
that her daughter was a perfectionist, and if she couldn't do something
perfectly, she wouldn't even try. Anytime Amanda didn't understand
a class assignment, she sat at her desk and cried. This really concerned
the mother because she remembered feeling the exact same way at that
age. The mother's own anxiety level skyrocketed as Amanda begged
her each morning not to send her to school. Mom had a choice at this
point: talk to the teacher and possibly obtain academic support for
Amanda or allow her to stay home. Unfortunately, Amanda's mom
chose the latter.

Because of her own anxiety as a child, this mom's parental anxiety
kicked in big time. She allowed her daughter to stay home for a week,
which turned into two. She made sure Amanda completed homework
assignments she picked up from the teacher but resisted the school's
insistence that Amanda return to class. It was only when she was told
that her daughter was at risk for repeating second grade that the mom
agreed to send her back. With extra support and attention from the
teacher, Amanda began to feel more comfortable and was able to complete her class assignments and school year.

Amanda began to do much better socially and academically, but
her mother did not. Because of her own heightened anxiety about her
daughter and strong desire that Amanda never have to suffer with anxiety as she had as a child, the mom began to make every effort to create
a stress-free life for her daughter. Anytime Amanda was hesitant to

attend a birthday party or activity, worrying she might not know all of the kids, her mom would either tell her she didn't have to go or she'd go out of her way to ensure that Amanda would feel comfortable if she attended. For example, the mom would call ahead to find out who'd be attending. She'd then call several of the girls' parents and offer to drive them so that Amanda would have friends with her when she arrived. If Amanda worried about a test, her mom let her stay home the day of the test and wrote an absence note the following morning stating that Amanda wasn't feeling well and to please allow her to take a makeup test.

By the time I saw Amanda, she was preparing to enter middle school. The week before, when I met with Mom, she told me that Amanda had seemed much less anxious over the past year but that she knew that the transition to middle school would be tough for her, just as her transition to elementary school had been. During my first session with Amanda, she told me she was a bit nervous but excited to finally being going to the middle school. Her nervousness was certainly appropriate for her new transition. A few weeks later, I discovered that Amanda's mom was much more nervous about Amanda entering middle school than Amanda was, to the point that she'd already been to the middle school on several occasions over the summer, asking them to please make sure that Amanda had a close friend in each of her seven classes. She also requested that Amanda be assigned a lunch period with several friends. The mom had even provided the guidance counselor with a detailed list of suggested friends for each class and lunch.

After learning this, I looked at Mom and said, "I know you are doing this out of love for your daughter, but you're actually doing her a disservice. The message you're sending Amanda is you don't believe she can handle this on her own."

The mom began to cry. She admitted that she didn't want her daughter to suffer as she had and was willing to do whatever it took so that Amanda felt comfortable. I reminded her that in her attempt to ensure that Amanda didn't suffer, she was preparing the path for her child rather than preparing Amanda for the path.

When we allow our parental anxiety to guide our parenting decisions, we're quick to jump in and fix just about any perceived "problem" with or for our children. We do this to calm our own anxiety. We continue the cycle of *fear . . . fix . . . fear . . . fix* parenting. I often refer to this as "whack a mole" parenting. Remember the kids' game where little moles pop their head up out of a hole and you whack them quickly back into place? As the game proceeds, the moles begin to pop up at a faster rate. Just as you get one in place, another little head appears. If you've ever played this game, you probably remember anticipating the mole's surprise head pop. As hard as you try, it becomes more difficult to keep them in their place. The same is true when we parent from a state of anxiety. In doing so, we become overwhelmed by trying to keep our kids and their lives in place. When we hover over our children in an attempt to ensure they never have to struggle, we actually prevent them from experiencing life and the essential lessons it offers. We believe we're doing it in service of our child, but in reality, we're doing it to serve our own needs—our needs to feel less anxious and more worthy as a parent.

Now, just as in the case of Amanda and her mother, we can see that anxiety is contagious and can negate or deny the respect and trust we try to build with our children. We overwhelm our nervous system when we allow our parental anxiety to take hold. When we anticipate a problem our children might face, our fight-or-flight survival mechanism kicks into gear, even when there is little or no danger. When your child runs out into a busy street, of course you need to react quickly in order to assure their safety! But not when they refuse to eat their dinner. Your underlying fear and associated thoughts may convince you otherwise.

For example, some moms fear their child will "starve" if they refuse to eat their dinner and go to bed hungry that night. This fear is only reinforced by their child's cry at bedtime—*but I'm starving* (as they plead for a snack or dessert). As a result, many moms end up routinely making their child a separate dinner in order to avoid their child's refusal to eat or the ensuing meltdown—a routine that moms often wish they'd never started. Your child may go to bed hungry (although most kids have had a late afternoon snack, so they aren't even hungry at dinnertime), but they won't starve. Your fear of starving your child or perhaps feeling like a bad mother prevents you from parenting rationally.

Hal Runkel suggests parenting from your parenting principles, not from your parental anxiety. Just imagine how that might shift your relationship with your child. It will almost guarantee better results in your child's behavior. No longer will you feel the need to fix, coerce, or cajole your child into behaving responsibly. When you give your child power over your own emotions, by saying *Don't make me angry* or *I need you to go to bed right this minute or else* (Or else you might have a meltdown yourself?), you lose your parenting power.

However, as long as you continue to parent from your own anxious place and in your effort to calm your own parental anxiety, you'll need your children to behave. Wanting children to behave so that they grow up to be responsible citizens is important. However, trying to coerce them into behaving in order to validate who you are as a parent is another. It's because of our very efforts to ensure our children become responsible and act accordingly that we end up we making our children responsible for our emotions. We need them to be a certain way in order to calm ourselves. We do this without even realizing it. But it's not our children's responsibility to take care of our emotions! It's their responsibility to learn to manage their own. They need us to control and manage our emotions so that we can then teach them to manage theirs. Anytime a child is tasked with handling their parent's emotions, there is a codependent relationship. Codependency occurs when our emotions and perceived well-being depend on the other person in the relationship. When one person in the relationship changes their way of being or compromises their values to avoid rejection or anger, there is codependency. In order to feel loved and safe, one conforms for another. You may have done this as a child. In order to please your parent or to ensure their happiness, you went along with their wishes. Maybe you became the "perfect" child. You may feel you lost yourself, or at least put another's emotional needs before your own. Unless you've healed your childhood wounds, there is a good chance you're taking your codependent nature into your adult relationships. Codependency plagues many marriages and parent-child relationships. When there is a codependent relationship between a parent and child, the parent's emotional needs become the perceived responsibility of the child. This is a huge responsibility to give to a child. Children are not equipped to take this responsibility on, nor should they be expected to do so.

If any of the following signs of a codependent relationship resonate with you, please take this opportunity to delve deeper into your history and current relationships. You learned it from your parents, and they learned it from theirs. Codependency is a generational issue and legacy, one you can easily pass on to your own child if unaware. According to Darlene Lancer, marriage and family therapist and codependency relationship expert, the following signs are indicative of a codependent relationship:

- Being overly focused on someone or something
- Low self-esteem
- Nonassertive communication
- Denying or devaluing needs, feelings, and wants
- Poor boundaries
- A need for control[41]

As a result of codependency, you are likely to want to be in control and will be quick to solve your kid's problems for them. You'll also depend on your child to meet your own needs.

It's important to not place this emotional burden on your child. Here are some ways to break the cycle of codependency in your family:

- Encourage open, healthy communication in the family.
  - Respect your child's feelings and thoughts.
  - Do not minimize what they've communicated by discounting what they've said.

- "Oh, you don't really mean that . . . or you don't really feel that way."
- By doing so, they will learn not to trust their own thoughts and feelings.

🕊 Do not try to keep family secrets.
  - If their father is an alcoholic, for example, encourage them to talk about this.

🕊 Respect your child's boundaries by:
  - Respecting their feelings.
  - Respecting their privacy by knocking before you enter their bedroom or bathroom; avoid snooping in their diary, mail, or email.
  - Listening to your child if they ask you to stop tickling them; their body is an important boundary and they should be allowed to set boundary limits. Telling you to stop tickling them empowers your child to tell others not to touch them inappropriately.

🕊 Empower your child to be responsible and make age-appropriate decisions.
  - In codependent relationships, children are interdependent with their parent and have difficulty making decisions. Allow your child the freedom and guidance to help them make the best decision for themselves.

🕊 Create reasonable rules and appropriate consequences.
  - In codependent families, there are either few rules that are inconsistently reinforced or strict, rigid rules.
  - While a child needs structure and limits, they also should have room to make choices and learn through their mistakes by experiencing the consequence of their choices.

- Demonstrate love and affection in your family; do not make it conditional on your child's behavior.
- Show empathy for your child.

Keep in mind that respect for your child is a big part of breaking the cycle of codependency. It's important to respect their communication and boundaries. It's also essential that you don't intrude on their privacy or decision-making. As your kids grow into their teen years, this becomes even more important.

Social media has certainly contributed to this challenge for parents, adding another area for us to wonder how much to monitor or respect our kid's activity online—especially because now the whole world can see how our children are behaving. In some ways, social media has become the new online diary for teens, and there are some things that parents are better off not knowing. I'm not promoting free rein for your child without any parental guidance. But just as you shouldn't violate your teen's privacy by reading their diary, I don't believe it's healthy or wise to read all of their social media posts. Besides violating their privacy, you also encourage them to become much better at hiding things from you. I've actually seen teens' behavior worsen when parents continually search their texts, emails, and social media accounts.

As wonderful as phone GPS tracking devices are, again, maybe you were never supposed to be able to follow their every move. Can you imagine how your life might have been different as teen if your parent had the ability to keep such a close eye on you? Parents have gone to all lengths to block accounts, monitor posts, and keep track of their children's whereabouts in an effort to keep them safe. Although it's important to set guidelines for your teen and discuss safety and negative consequences of inappropriate online behavior, it's also important to allow your child space: space to learn to be responsible for themselves. If they choose to post a mean-spirited comment about a classmate on social media, which gets back to the school, resulting in school detention, allow your teen to experience the consequence of their action. Knowing the school's no-bullying policy and still choosing to post the negative post is a choice your child made. You were not aware of their decision, and you are certainly not responsible for it. Your kid's behavior in social media posts is not a reflection of your parenting ability but are more about the way he is choosing to represent himself.

Feeling and Managing Your Emotions

It's as if my children are awakening in me repressed hurts and fears that I don't wish to feel. It's far easier to detach, fix, coerce, manage, or abandon ship than it is to simply be present. However, if I'm not willing to own my fears and emotions, my children must continue to act them out on my behalf. While at times it's a tough pill to swallow, the more I accept the above to be true, the more harmony and joy fills our family.

—*Luma, father of two*

Your ability to feel, express, and manage your emotions determines your own emotional intelligence. It also affects your child's ability to manage their own. Children act out their parents' own unresolved emotional issues. Your most "difficult" child has the power to help you become aware and resolve your emotional wounds. Yes, the child who pushes your buttons on a daily basis—the one you most struggle with—is the one who will potentially teach you the most about yourself. Children challenge you to grow. To become the adult, the parent, they want and need you to be—a parent who's able to stop, self-reflect, and take responsibility for themselves instead of a parent who needs their child to behave in order to feel good about herself. Your children will continue to challenge you and push your buttons. As Hal Runkel states, "I hope they continue to push your buttons—for your own growth." He adds, "Growth is optional—your choice." I assure you, your kids are asking you to grow.

In order to grow, it's imperative to recognize and heal your own unresolved emotions, as we discussed in the previous chapter. This is the best gift you can give your children. When you become more aware and accepting of your own emotions—the good, the bad, and the ugly—you'll become more accepting of your children's emotions.

> For "full" emotional communication, one person needs to allow his state of mind to be influenced by that of the other.
>
> —*Dr. Dan Siegel*, The Developing Mind

Can you be the one who is calm in spite of how your child is behaving? Your child needs you to be there to help guide them through their emotional upheavals. However, to be able to do this, you must first be able to handle your own emotions. Parents often tell me that when their child or teen is emotionally out of control, they feel the same way. They admit to either suppressing their own emotions (out of fear of losing it), allowing them to fester, or letting loose in an emotionally big way. At this point, both the child and parent are out of control! Suppressing your emotions or exploding does not serve you or your child.

Expecting your child to remain calm while you're out of control also does not work. Remember that your actions speak volumes. Your credibility as a parent is on the line when you yourself lose control of your emotions. In the past, when you've become as reactive as your child, has that helped or hindered the situation? Most parents realize early on that their out-of-control behavior has helped only to fuel their child's explosive behavior.

I've worked with parents who'd previously been referred for anger management classes. Although the class tried to teach them to *manage* their anger, most I've worked with have learned to squelch their anger or distract themselves from their inner feelings. Rather than trying to manage your anger, why not give yourself the time and space to feel what you're feeling? (Often, something else is brewing long before the anger arises—sadness, fear, jealousy, resentment.) By allowing yourself to feel the underlying feelings, you may discover that it actually takes less of your energy than trying to manage your anger. Allowing yourself to feel an emotion helps to dissipate the strong hold it has had on you. Feelings that are acknowledged, accepted, and not quickly pushed away have less power over you. It's your resistance to feel the emotion and just *be* with it that keeps it around longer. I like to think of "unwanted" emotions as little kids crying out, "Look at me . . . look at me . . . hey, look at me!" And the more you resist them, the longer and louder they cry. Your emotional patterns and behavior are signaling you to pay attention. Your courage to examine what lies beneath will help serve to release old patterns—ultimately leading to your emotional freedom!

Journaling Exercises

Before exploring ways to help you express and manage your emotions, take some time to reflect on the journaling exercises. Be courageous, honest, and gentle with yourself. You've probably harbored these emotions for a very long time. It's okay if you're not sure of their origin. What matters is that you're able to identify them and do not try to run away from them. Do this for yourself and your child.

- As a child, were you encouraged to express your feelings? Were all your feelings or only some of them permitted?

- Did you find it easy or difficult to express how you were feeling as you were growing up?

◈   How did your mother express her feelings? Your father?

◈   In your family, were there any spoken or unspoken messag-
    es related to expression of feelings? Were you allowed to be
    angry?

◈   Reflect on a childhood incident that angered you—one that
    you still think about as an adult. I would suggest initially
    choosing one that was not traumatic in nature (abusive or
    neglectful); it could be an incident that occurred at school, at
    any place outside of your home, or within your family.

◈   Can you identify one feeling associated with this incident? If
    so, spend the next few minutes in a quiet space. Close your
    eyes, take some deep breaths, and then breathe slowly into that
    feeling. If you find yourself distracted or triggered, continue to
    slow your breathing. Breathe in and out slowly. Allow your-
    self to feel the sadness, resentment, fear, or anger. Allow the
    feeling to just be, without the need to fix it, push it away, or be
    distracted from it. When you're finished, journal your experi-
    ence of allowing yourself just to be with the emotion.

When you suppress your emotions, at some point, they begin to leak
out—often in unhealthy ways. Your reactions become out of proportion to the incident. (Your child spills a glass of milk, and you go into
a tirade. You may have been feeling resentful and unappreciated as a
mother. You might feel overwhelmed because all the childcare and
household duties seem to fall to you. The spilled milk is the last straw
that just tips you over the edge.) It's not until you begin to uncover
your true feelings that you're then able to make positive changes in
the way you express and manage your emotions.

   Listed below are various strategies to help you learn to recognize
and express your emotions in a healthy manner:

- ꧁ Make a list of what triggers your emotions (what makes you sad, irritated, mad, etc.).
- ꧁ Journal about your emotions and associated triggers (e.g., Every time my child ignores me, I become angry).
- ꧁ Talk about your feelings with a friend, loved one, or professional.
- ꧁ Be aware if you become triggered while journaling or talking about your feelings; pause, breathe, and take a short break. It's okay to feel what you're feeling. Simply by doing this, you will begin to notice when your feelings show up.
- ꧁ Remind yourself that your thoughts, if held tightly, become your beliefs (e.g., My child is an angry child; each time your child becomes angry, this encourages you to see this as proof and hold onto your belief).
- ꧁ Know that emotions are transient—they do not last forever, neither sadness nor joy.
- ꧁ Begin feeling and expressing the least threatening emotion. (I am sad or frustrated is less emotionally charged than I am angry.)

Managing your emotions takes practice. You learn to flex your emotional muscles. Every day you're given an opportunity to pause and ask yourself, *What am I feeling in this moment?*

Creating the Calm Within

Although it's important to discover hidden feelings that trigger emotional reactivity, it's also vital to learn to calm yourself down in the moment. That's easier said than done sometimes. Being able to calm yourself down is a skill that takes time and practice to develop. There has been a lot written about how to create a state of calm in our lives, and there are many tips and suggestions as to how to do this. Although many of these tips found in books, in magazines, and on the Internet are helpful, one size doesn't fit all. It's up to you to find what works for you and to realize that finding your place of calm comes from your intention and willingness to practice.

Calming yourself down becomes easier after you've taken a moment (or two) to pause. This pause allows you the space to slow your overstimulated and overreactive nervous system down.

Here are some calming techniques you may find helpful:

- Stop and create a pause. The pause will create a space between what triggered you and your emotional reactivity.
- Take three calming breaths—inhaling through your nose and exhaling through your mouth—each to the count of four.
- Continue to slowly breathe in and out as you notice your body and brain begin to relax. This will help to calm your sympathetic nervous system and lessen the release of stress hormones, adrenaline, and cortisol.
- If possible, remove yourself from the situation; take five minutes to allow yourself to calm down.
- Do something physical which will help reduce and release the "fight or flight" adrenaline buildup in your body.
- Include calming activities in your daily life, such as walking, running, yoga, or meditation.

By incorporating calming techniques into your day, you will begin to retrain your body and brain. Rather than remaining in the continuous fear-react cycle, you'll teach your body and brain to inhabit a calm-respond way of being.

Besides creating calm moments each day, whether it be by taking a walk, meditation, deep breathing, or a bubble bath, you help yourself identify ways to calm yourself in the moment.

Remember, the first step is to become aware of what you're feeling when you're triggered. Are you scared, angry, or frustrated? Acknowledge that first. When a parent becomes angry without pausing and acknowledging their anger, they ignore or sometimes or even deny it. The parent quickly reacts and blames their child for making them angry. We often jump into reactivity without even realizing what we're feeling. Until you recognize it, feel it, and allow it, trying to make it go away is next to impossible. Becoming a ScreamFree Parent, according to Hal Runkel, is possible when you try to create a pause between stimulus and response as you learn to calm yourself down. The shift from your own reactivity to your ability to respond will benefit you and your kids! When your teen tells you to *chill out*, that is exactly what they're asking you to do.

Check Your Thoughts; Check Your Actions

Our thoughts help create our reality. The saying "What we think, we believe, and then act upon" is true. Our thoughts and beliefs provide a lens through which we see our children. We create perceptions about our children that may or may not be true. And our actions are based on our perceptions.

> We're only ever one new thought away from a completely different experience.
>
> —*Michael Neill*, The Inside-Out Revolution

Each day, each moment, you're given an opportunity as a parent to choose a different thought, a thought that will change how you experience your child. Perhaps instead of automatically assuming your daughter or son is strong-willed and defiant, first pause and calm yourself down. Consider the possibility that your child is tenacious and goal oriented. They're driven to go after what they want. Not bad character traits for them to possess. It certainly will serve them well as an adult, as long as they've learned how to use their will appropriately during childhood. And they will learn this as a result of your calm and loving guidance.

As their teacher, your calm demeanor and actions speak much louder than your emotional reactivity. Your child will learn best through their experience, rather than words. As noted before, you are your child's first role model, and they are watching and learning from you. They watch how you handle your own emotions—do you express them in a calm, clear manner, or are you easily angered? Are you compassionate or judgmental when triggered? Again, your child learns from their experience of you. Telling them to "do as I say, not as I do" does not work and is not an effective way to teach. Children are wise and see right through the way you conduct yourself on a daily basis.

The words you use when teaching your child to express and manage their own emotions do matter. Notice the difference in the following scenario.

A child begins to cry, and her mother, out of frustration, says, "Stop crying. Crying is for babies! You're a big girl now."

What lesson does the little girl learn? Most likely that crying is not allowed or that she is bad because she can't control her emotions. She may also hear that she is too sensitive and needs to toughen up. We've all had our emotional expression tampered with at some point in our life. We've all been shamed for our emotions and behavior.

Now imagine how this little girl might have felt if her crying yielded a different response from her mother, such as, "You seem sad that Sophie doesn't want to play with you. Would you like to talk about it?"

Journaling Exercises

- ⚉   When you reflect on your relationship with your child, what emotions do you feel?

- ⚉   How would you describe your relationship with your child?

- ⚉   Can you identify any patterns in your relationship? What is your part of the pattern?

How do these patterns affect you? Your child? Choose a pattern (e.g., your child begins to cry and you tell them to stop or they'll be sent to their room) and begin to explore ways in which you could shift this pattern toward a more positive direction.

Identify patterns and habits that have been created within the relationship that may have a negative impact on the child and their behavior.

Recognize your own way of being in the relationship and the impact that it has on your child's behavior. (Are you present and attentive or distracted? Are you calm or quick to anger?)

Begin to think of new ways to create healthy connections with your child (e.g., take a walk at night and look at the stars. Create a feelings journal with your child; encourage them to express how they're feeling. You can also use the journal to communicate with each other.)

Helping Your Child Manage Their Emotions

When your child feels connected to you, they are more open to learn from you. Through connection, you have the opportunity to model how you manage your emotions in a healthy manner. And you're also given the opportunity to teach your child how to manage their own. This teaching occurs more readily when you allow and accept *all* of your child's emotions. Research has shown that when parents are more accepting of their child's expansive range of emotions, the child learns to accept and manage their own emotions. They also learn to accept and love themselves.

Children are emotional little beings and express their feelings quite naturally—unless we teach them not to. An infant's cry is their emotional language, as is cooing and giggling. They naturally express what they're feeling. If you've spent much time with a toddler, you've observed how they delight in life's simple pleasures (watching bubbles in the air, making silly faces, chasing a butterfly flitting past them) but also how they can quickly become frustrated and dissolve into tears. Toddlers express their excitement and their upset in a big way! A toddler's laugh can be infectious and their frustration frightening.

As parents, we often do everything in our power to keep the peace. In the process, though, we sometimes shut down our children's emotions. We're not even aware of what we're doing. We tell them to stop crying, whining, or throwing their toys in a fit of anger. We attempt to distract or punish them. But toddlers communicate through their emotions and behavior. They've not yet developed the capacity to handle their own emotions. Expecting a toddler to "just stop crying" is unrealistic and often fuels their fire. The same is true for children and teens, depending on their temperament and developmental stage.

One of the most important lessons you can teach your child is how to *be* with their emotions. A child's ability to understand and express their emotions varies from child to child. You may have one child who seems to go with the flow, while another is easily set off. This difference is explained in part by their temperament—the disposition they were born with. Being able to discern between your child's inability to manage their emotions and the willful use of their emotions in a manipulative manner is an important task in parenting—yet not an easy one. You might quickly assume that your child is throwing a temper tantrum to get what they want; however, your child may simply not have the capacity to calm themselves. And, let's be

SAD

It's all blue.
You keep falling.
You were hurt by your heart.
You can't stop yourself from falling.
You fall into a dark hole.
You feel unlucky.
You are SAD.

—Olive

honest: some adults struggle with this, too. Maybe they didn't feel heard or understood as a child. They may have grown up in a family where emotions weren't discussed and were to be kept hidden. Yelling or physical force was how they learned to be seen or heard.

Telling a child to go to their room may teach them to stop crying, but it doesn't help them learn to express and regulate their emotions if you don't help them process their emotions once they've calmed down. What they learn is that what they're feeling is not okay. The same holds true for ignoring them when throwing a tantrum or crying. Certainly you don't want to enable the behavior by giving into a tantrum, but telling your child "I'm here for you if you need me" (by offering a hug or your willingness to sit down and talk) lets them know that you see their pain. Through your willingness to allow your child to feel their own feelings, you help them move through their emotions rather than stuffing them below the surface. Can you imagine how the world might be a different place if we all had learned to feel and heal our own emotions?

Do you ever wonder what your child is feeling? Not based on the emotional outburst they're clearly showing you, but what lies beneath? Most likely your child is not able to express their feelings in the heat of the moment, but chances are in the quiet of the night they reflect on how those big emotions made them feel. I recently asked my nine-year-old granddaughter and poet to share her thoughts about feelings—and what kids would like their parents to know. She reminds us that feelings can be jumbled and confusing for kids as well as parents:

MAD

When you are mad you feel red.
You feel like being mad would help.
All the pink and yellow turns into black and red.
Your candle turns off.
Your being stops.
You don't think.
All there is in your head is screaming.
That is what MAD means.

—Olive

Kid's Feelings

by Olive

We get sad . . . mad . . . happy . . . excited . . . angry . . . scared and surprised. But sometimes our parents don't know. And sometimes that changes our feelings. If you could feel a color when you are sad is would be blue. As a kid when you are sad it's like a twist of sad and mad. Sometimes you are sad but you don' talk you show it as mad. We feel lonely . . . like we're the only one. You feel like you need help. Your heart drops. You can't talk. Sometimes you get mad. Your body feels like fire. You think hurting and taking. But when you get mad you just hurt you.

When you are happy it's like balloons are floating around you. But sometimes we get to happy and something goes wrong. But mostly it's gold. Sometimes we get excited . . . it's just a bigger happiness. Same in angry. Just with mad. When you get scared you might get sad too. We have feelings and that changes the WORLD.

When you model for your child how you handle your own emotions in a healthy manner, you teach them to be comfortable experiencing and regulating their own emotions. They will carry this invaluable lesson with them throughout their lives. Here are some simple ways to instill their learning:

- Let your child know that all emotions are accepted in the family.
- Acknowledge their feelings and set limits.
- Address your child's unmet needs and underlying feelings.
- Remember that anger is a disguise for sadness, fear, or hurt.
- If you have to say no, if possible, figure out a way to say yes.

⊛ Don't take your child's behavior personally—and resist the temptation to defend yourself.

Journaling Exercises

⊛ How easy or hard is it for you to allow and accept your child's emotions?

⊛ Are there any particular emotions that are more difficult for you to accept? If so, why? How do you react or respond to your child's emotions?

⊛ Have you noticed how your reaction affects your child's ability to manage their emotions? If so, how?

⊛ Knowing what I know now, I intend to . . .

Chapter 8

Discipline Is Not a Dirty Word

Where did we ever get the crazy idea
that in order to make children do better,
first we have to make them feel worse?
Think of the last time you felt humiliated
or treated unfairly. Did you feel like
cooperating or doing better?

—Jane Nelsen, *Positive Discipline*

*m*ost mothers recognize the importance of discipline. Most also believe that it's a parent's job to provide it. But many struggle with how to incorporate discipline in their daily parenting, discipline that helps guide their children toward becoming responsible and caring individuals. Before examining the "how to" of discipline, I'd like to make the distinction that any discipline that is punitive or causes harm is not discipline. My observation has been that the word *discipline* seems to have taken on a negative connotation. Some parents view discipline as a way to keep their kids in line. Other parents have told me, "I don't want to be the disciplinarian in my family like my father (or mother) was. I want to teach my child in a kinder way." Dr. Daniel Siegel points out that the word *discipline* comes from the word *disciple*, meaning *student, pupil, and learner.*[42] To discipline is to teach. Your undertaking (or job) as a parent is to teach and guide your child into responsible adulthood, all the while honoring them as unique individuals. However, your method of teaching can either encourage or diminish your child.

Chapter Summary

Discipline has taken on a negative connotation. It is often confused with punishment or an attempt to control a child's behavior. Often, mothers resort to using manipulation or control—in its most negative sense—to manage their child's behavior. Children resist being controlled, just as we do as adults. Some children may comply, but this typically lasts temporarily, often bringing a mother right back to her original frustration. The vicious cycle continues until mothers begin to examine why their way of disciplining is not working. Once they've identified the problem and discovered what will actually help improve their child's behavior, they can consciously choose to discipline in a different way. By shifting their perspective, moms begin to realize that there is a different way, a better way, to teach children.

Discipline—What It Is and What It's Not

So what is discipline, and how can you provide it for your kids? First, by reminding yourself that your child is not their behavior. Shefali Tsabary, PhD, author of *Out of Control: Why Disciplining Your Child Doesn't Work—and What Will*, states, "When we engage with our children from the belief that child discipline is a vital aspect of our role as parents, we assume children are inherently undisciplined and need to be civilized."[43] We then believe it's our job to ensure our children behave accordingly. This belief perpetuates a parent's thought process that it is their job to keep their kids under control. And in order to do this, they must employ a system of disciplinary tactics. Demands, threats, punishment, and rewards become the daily artillery parents use to attempt to fix or control their kid's behavior. I use the word *artillery* intentionally. Parents often tell me that they're constantly struggling with their kids. And they are—usually in an attempt to gain power and control. I've overheard parents saying, "Well, I won that battle, but hopefully, I'll also win the war." They're referring to power struggles with their kids.

So the cycle continues—demands, threats, punishment, and rewards. The child increasingly resists being controlled, while the parents believe they must exert more control. You can employ the best disciplinary tactics and your kids will still test the limits, especially if they feel micromanaged and controlled.

But if we substituted the word *teach* for *discipline*, how might this help shift the focus of discipline? Would parents no longer feel the need to control their child's behavior? After all, whose behavior problem is it anyway? Children learn more about themselves and how to interact with others when you are there to help guide them—calmly—when you're the parent who sets limits and holds your child accountable for their actions. The operative word is *guidance*, not control.

Discipline is as an integral part of mindful parenting. It's not a quick fix or a one size fits all. Each kid is different. Discipline is a process, based on acceptance, connection, and guidance.

We've discussed that you share a part of the behavioral equation (your own parental anxiety, reactions, and expectations). Some mothers who are aware of their own behavioral contribution and make necessary changes in themselves often expect their child's behavior to immediately improve. When it doesn't, they resort once again to using control to manage their children's behavior. Some kids comply, but typically their compliance is short lived, quickly bringing a mother right back to her original frustration. Typically, I get a call when moms have run out of disciplinary tactics. This vicious cycle continues until mothers take time to examine why their discipline isn't working. When they're able to shift their perspective, they begin to realize there's a different way—a better way—to discipline (teach) children. There are many ways to discipline (teach) with many positive outcomes. But before we discuss those tactics, I'd like to talk about the many reasons children behave the way they do.

Your child's behavior occurs for a reason—it's not random. Take some time to let that sink in. You may have observed that your child becomes increasingly irritable during certain times of the day. Some children's irritability is triggered by hunger or fatigue. Consequently, their resulting meltdown is not a random occurrence but rather directly related to lack of food or sleep.

But some children's behavioral triggers aren't as obvious. They're more covert. This is particularly true for children who melt down frequently. I've worked with many parents who are baffled by their child's behavior. They often tell me there's no rhyme or reason for their child's erratic behavior. I assure them, as I assure you, that there's a reason, but it may not be obvious. There may be underlying feelings that need to be addressed. Often, children who feel invisible in the family will act out to get attention. Because they do not feel seen or heard, they feel powerless. Some children are emotionally sensitive and become easily overwhelmed by life. Once parents are willing to explore and gain a better understanding of their child's behavior, they often begin to discover the root cause. The parent begins to understand that the way they previously handled their child's behavior actually increased the likelihood of its occurrence.

Before I assist parents in their "search and discovery" process in an effort to better understand their child's behavior, I invite them first to examine their own. Some parents resist the idea that their own behavior directly affects their child's. They continue to focus on their child rather than themselves. After all, they've consulted me to fix their child's behavior, not their own. Suggesting a parent focus on their own behavior contradicts most parenting books. I am not saying that your behavior is causing your child's behavior problem, but it's certainly connected to it. When there are repeated behavioral patterns, you are a part of the pattern. When you tell your child to put their shoes on over and over, to no avail, you are helping to create this pattern. And when you yell at them for not listening to you the first time, you reinforce this pattern.

Focusing on and trying to control your child's behavior will not help them learn. As long as you continue to focus on your child's "mis"behavior and employ disciplinary tactics to stop the behavior, you contribute to the problem. How might your child's behavior change if you altered your approach and asked yourself the following three questions, created by Dr. Siegel?

- Why did my child act this way?
- What lesson do I want to teach in this moment?
- How can I best teach this lesson?[44]

These three questions alone can begin to shift the way you discipline (teach) and interact with your child.

The art of discipline (it's an art, not a science) has been confused with punishment. Although most parents agree that children should be taught to behave, there seems to be uncertainty as to how to do this. I believe the missing links in discipline are connection and guidance.

In an effort to discipline and ensure children behave, parents often resort to control. Parents worry that if their child isn't disciplined, they'll misbehave, especially children who push limits. When a child misbehaves, some parents strengthen their disciplinary tactics and exert more control over their kids. This only serves to ramp up their child's resistance. Remember: no one likes to be controlled. Dr. Tsabary states, "Their resistance, or at best half-heartedness, intensifies the parental need to control, as the parent bears down on the child, believing the stricter they are the more the child will comply. It's this resistance that becomes emotional plaque, creating barriers to learning, growth, and—most of all—connection between the parent and child."[45] Even the most well-meaning parent is capable of unconsciously exerting control over a child, often with shame. Unintended shame, certainly, but shame nonetheless.

When your child misbehaves, pause for a moment before you say a word and ask yourself, *What do I want the outcome to be for my child?* Are you more concerned about your child's immediate behavior or what you hope they learn from their behavior? Are you feeling compelled to stop the behavior (to calm your own parental anxiety) or are you hoping to use the moment to teach him so that he will learn to manage his own behavior in the future? In the moment, most likely, you can't have both. Imagine how much simpler parenting would be if you didn't feel the need to stop your child's behavior, if you weren't on high alert ready to stamp out the misbehavior, even before it occurred. What if, instead, you inspired your child to choose appropriate behavior for themselves? And you accomplished this through connection and guidance? And you allowed them to experience the consequence of their own choices? In the long run, connection and guidance will be of greater importance than stopping misbehavior.

Journaling Exercises

☞   Were your parents strict or lenient? As a parent, are you more likely to parent as you were parented or differently? Why?

⚉ Trying to strike a balance between being a "strict" parent versus a "lenient" parent is not easy and takes a conscious effort. How do you parent most often?

⚉ If you are strict, or more controlling, as a parent, how does your parenting style affect your child?

⚉ How might your child's behavior change if you were able to loosen your control—to let go a bit?

⚉ If you're more lenient, how has your style of parenting affected your child's behavior in a positive or negative way?

⚉ Can you think of ways your child might benefit if you were to be less lenient?

Benefits of Disciplining (Teaching) Your Child

Do you teach your child in a manner that encourages and empowers them to learn to be responsible? Although you may have a fundamental understanding of your role as teacher, you might find your attention focused more on your child's misbehavior. You may also focus more on finding the most fitting punishment or consequence for your child's behavior, especially when you're frustrated or angry. Parents frequently ask me what consequences to use with their children because what they've tried so far hasn't worked. It's difficult to figure out what to do in the moment when your child refuses to get ready for bed, grabs their sister's doll for the fifth time in an hour, or slams the door in your face. Most likely your focus and goal at that moment is to put an end to their behavior. But what if you began to shift your focus? Focusing *less* on how to get your child to behave and *more* on what you want your child to learn from the experience?

Recently, I spoke with a dad of a ten-year-old boy. The father and son seemed to be engaged in an endless power struggle. The more the dad tried to stop his son's behavior, the more the son resisted. After several sessions with the father and son, I asked the dad what his overall parenting goals were. He quickly responded, "To get my son to listen to me. When I tell him to stop doing something, he needs to stop. And when I tell him he needs to do something, he should do it."

This dad's parenting goals were fairly common and not that unreasonable. But what was his son learning in the process? That dad got mad when he didn't comply. He also learned to wait until dad reminded him repeatedly and lost his temper—and then he begrudgingly complied. What he didn't learn was to make decisions for himself—and experience the consequences of his decision. He also didn't learn to think for himself when he wasn't around his dad. Of course, the dad wanted his son to behave well outside the home, but how could he ensure this would actually happen if he wasn't there to keep an eye on his son? He couldn't.

However, if he encouraged his son to make appropriate behavioral choices at home, there was a much better chance he would continue to do so even when his dad was not present. The piece that was missing between the dad and son was connection and the opportunity to teach skills that would enable the child to make appropriate decisions for himself in the future.

You wear several hats as a mom—nurturer, advocate, and caregiver. You'd also like to be the fun mom and friend, right? And you can, while providing guidance in a manner that nurtures and maintains connection with your child—guidance that provides boundaries for your child. Your ability to do so will enable your child to make responsible choices. Your children will also learn to be critical thinkers and problem-solvers. And best of all, they'll learn to honor themselves as they learn to make decisions for themselves.

Harsh discipline (punitive discipline) creates fear and is shame based. The resulting negative message for the child is *I'm bad and unworthy.* They don't learn from their mistakes. They usually only learn to behave in an effort to please you or to avoid the resulting punishment, but they don't learn for themselves. What you really want your child to learn is self-discipline. To be able to monitor their own behavior and decision-making—even when you're not present.

One of the most important benefits of providing discipline for your child is that they learn to discipline themselves. Self-discipline offers them the necessary tools to guide themselves through life, long after they've left your nest. And again, the key to providing and modeling discipline is through a loving connection. Positive discipline helps build children's self-esteem and improve their behavior.

So How Does Discipline (Teaching) Really Work?

> When we fail to set boundaries and hold people accountable, we feel used and mistreated. This is why we sometimes attack who they are, which is far more hurtful than addressing a behavior or a choice.
>
> —*Brené Brown*, The Gifts of Imperfection

Discipline works when you focus more on providing guidance for your child and less on trying to make them behave, when you devote your attention to ways to connect with your child rather than focusing on ways to punish them. Kids are much more apt to respect and listen to a parent when they feel connected. Although structure is important for your child, you should not create an impossibly rigid structure. There may be times when it's appropriate to bend the rules, but that should be the exception rather than the rule. Remember, you don't want to be the drill sergeant in the family or the wimpy parent. So don't bark orders or cave under pressure. Strive to be a calm, steady parent who focuses more on your own behavior and less on your child's.

Discipline works when you are crystal clear with your expectations. Vague expectations only create confusion. When you tell your child you expect them to be good, what does "be good" mean to your child? Be explicit with your request—"When we go into the store, please hold my hand." Create clear rules, but not too many. Too many rules create confusion for both parents and kids. And if a child feels restricted by too many rules, they resist. Simplify rules: safety first, personal responsibility, and family rules.

Discipline works when you acknowledge appropriate behavior instead of focusing on unwanted behavior. "Catch them being good" is a phrase we often use in therapy sessions. We all like to be acknowledged and rewarded for our efforts. When I speak of rewards, I'm not referring to purchasing a toy or latest gadget. I advise parents not to create the "gimme monster." This occurs when children choose appropriate behavior only if they know they will be rewarded. (And don't reward everything. Children need to recognize they are an important part of the family and can contribute by helping around the house. Don't use rewards all of the time to control your kid's behavior—life does not provide constant rewards.)

Discipline works when communication is healthy. Do not engage in arguments. If your child tries to engage you in an argument, acknowledge what they're saying or feeling—say "I know" or "I understand." Acknowledgment doesn't mean you have to agree with them. And when speaking to your child, remind yourself that less is more. The fewer words you speak, the louder your message will be. After acknowledging their feelings, get back on the task at hand by saying, "You know what you're supposed to do" or "And what did I say?" Acknowledge your child's anger: "I know you were mad when you hit Max. He broke your favorite toy. But remember, it's not okay to hit, so you're going to need to apologize to Max for hitting him." It's also important to help your child identify ways that they can handle the situation in a more positive way next time.

Discipline works when your kids can rely on you and know what to expect. Be consistent—or ridiculously consistent, as Hal Runkel suggests. It's easy to slack sometimes—to let your kids get away with stuff, especially when you're tired or don't have the energy to endure the consequences of their behavior (meltdowns can be exhausting for parents as well as kids). Your ability to be consistent also applies to rules and consequences you've created as well as promises you've made. Mean what you say and say what you mean. Your credibility is on the line. Your kids need to know that they can trust you to enforce the limits you've set. It's the structure and limits that help your child feel safe.

Discipline works when you're a good role model. Children learn by imitating others. Be careful about what you want your child to imitate. Keep in mind that you cannot curse in your child's presence and then expect them not to. You also cannot say mean-spirited things and then become upset when they throw a few mean-spirited comments your way.

And most importantly, *discipline really works* when you value love and connection with your child over trying to fix their behavior.

Yes, No, or Maybe?

I've worked with many parents who hate telling their child no. They fully understand the importance of saying no but fear the imminent emotional outburst when their child hears this word. There are some children who melt down quickly when told no—no to their plea for one more cookie, an afternoon playdate, or getting a new toy that is staring them in the face while in the toy store. Most kids just don't want to hear no. And some react more vehemently to no than others. If you have a child who has an aversion to no, do you find yourself tiptoeing around this word? Do you find yourself delaying your no by saying maybe instead? Or saying no while preparing to defend yourself? Perhaps you even armor yourself to protect your own emotions. Kids have to be told no sometimes—there is no way around it.

However, there are different ways to say it—ways to encourage open communication. The power of no, yes, and maybe lies in the delivery. Saying "No, you can't go to Jack's house. I already told you we're going to the mall . . . now stop your whining" only serves to intensify your child's frustration and anger. A no is still a no, but when delivered with empathy, it encourages the likelihood your child will be more willing to listen. Perhaps next time, try saying something like "I know you're disappointed you can't have a playdate with Jack. Right now is not a good time, so let's figure out a time that is and we'll give Jack's mom a call." I remind parents to say yes more frequently than no—but don't avoid saying no.

When you tell your child yes, no, or maybe, do you actually mean what you say? Is the word congruent with your truth? Or have these words lost their significance? Perhaps you say no but are worn down by your child's ensuing meltdown, so you cave and say yes. Although you may not speak the word *yes*, your actions shout yes. What actually might come out of your mouth is, "Fine, go ahead—I don't care!" Remember that kids want what they want and are tenacious little beings. They don't give up easily, especially when they've learned that if they wear you down, you will say yes. If you're not in alignment with your own integrity, why then should your kids be? If you're willing to fold under pressure when your teen misses her curfew for the third time, why should she be concerned about the curfew to begin with? Your kids will challenge your integrity and your word on a daily basis, even though they're ultimately hoping you won't cave to the challenge.

Some parents say yes in an effort to just keep the peace. Some mothers who struggle with saying no to others in their life also struggle with saying it to their child. In order to please others, they say yes. In order to go along with what other parents do or what kids expect, they say yes. Kids will always want something they don't have: the latest gadget, phone, electronic device, or whatever their friends have. When parents give into their child's demands while feeling uneasy about their decision, most likely they're not in alignment with their own beliefs. When you say yes, make sure you mean it. If you tell your daughter yes to taking her shopping with a friend when you're still upset with her for her behavior last night, your yes will carry negative energy. Rather than taking her shopping while still holding a grudge, address the behavior first.

When you're aware of your intentions in saying yes or no, you're much more likely to say it with confidence. You will not waffle when your child tries to wear you down—and over time, they will learn to accept and trust your answer. An arbitrary yes or no will only confuse your kids. Saying yes to the new puppy (that you really don't want but feel you should give into) will likely result in your frustration—especially if you had the expectation that your child would take care of the puppy on their own. Yes, they promised they would, but without having the conversation about the importance of caring for animals and consequence of not doing so, you find yourself taking care of the puppy yourself. Perhaps your yes was not aligned with your reality. It was said in an effort to please your child or simply keep the peace.

The same goes for saying no. When you say no, do it because it aligns with your integrity as a parent. Otherwise, you may second-guess yourself when your child continues to badger you in an effort to get you to change your mind. I've worked with many children who tell me that when their parents say no, they know their parents don't really mean it. If the parents don't really believe their own no, why should their kids? Recently, I overheard a teen in a restaurant talking with a friend about an upcoming party. She complained that her parents told her she couldn't go. But then she went on to assure her friend that she'd be able to go because her parents always gave in at the last minute. "I just refuse to talk to them, and then they finally give in—it works every time." I secretly wished I could let this girl's parents in on her secret (although they're likely aware—just worn down).

Although a maybe doesn't guarantee a yes, most kids remain hopeful, to the point that they often translate the maybe into a yes. My advice is to use maybe sparingly and never use it to delay or soften a no. Whether you say yes or no, say it with confidence—confident that you made this decision based on your truth. By doing so, you'll teach

your child the value of your word. Although they may not be happy
with your decision, they'll learn to trust that you mean what you say.
No matter how much they try to wear you down, your ability to set
limits help them feel safe and secure.

They know they can trust you as their parent. How your child responds to you is up to them. Again, you cannot and should not try to
control their behavior, but it's up to you to set consequences related
to their behavior.

Drama-Free Discipline

Discipline without drama? Yes, it's possible. The premise of *No-
Drama Discipline*, coauthored by Daniel Siegel, MD, and Tina Payne
Bryson, PhD, is to discipline by connecting and redirecting. When
you're quick to react to your child's behavior, there's no time for connection. Connection, as we've discussed, is a vital component in your
relationship with your child. It's also related to your child's behavior. Your child is much more likely to cooperate with you if they first
feel connected to you. And your reactive threats, punishments, and
over-the-top consequences (created out of anger) will only serve to
further the disconnect while worsening both their behavior and your
relationship with them. For example, if you say, "Don't kick your
sister . . . that's it . . . you've lost your video games for a week!," you
inflame your child's frustration and anger, prompting them to lash
out again. Out of your own frustration and anger, you lash out with
another punishment (often harsher than the first), and the cycle continues. What has your child learned? The drama in this approach
results from your own reactivity (yelling, giving over-the-top consequences or those with no connection to the behavior, spanking,
grounding) and your child's (more yelling, hitting, door slamming).

We connect with our children in many different ways. You're
more likely to connect with your child when they're happy, easygo-
ing, and behaving. It's easier to connect then, right? Your challenge
is to connect with them when you feel like turning your back and

running away—or when you want to banish them from the family. When was the last time you wanted to push your child away? Perhaps they were angry and lashing out at you. Maybe you told them no and had to endure a major meltdown in public. Chances are they were emotionally overwhelmed and targeted their anger toward you. Your immediate reaction may have been to put them in their place, to try to control or stop their behavior. In that overwhelming moment, that's exactly the time to *pause*, get curious about their behavior, and connect. Connection can only occur when you're calm and aware, when you intentionally pause and pay attention. You're then able to listen to, respect, and communicate with your child. Although you may not understand or agree with your child's behavior or emotions, you'll be more willing to accept them as they are in that moment. This is when connection occurs.

> We can either meet children's needs for connection or we can spend our time dealing with the unmet need behaviors. Either way, we spend the time.
>
> —*Pam Leo*, Connection Parenting

Connection does not preclude limit-setting or boundaries. Actually, it often requires it! You'll still hold your child responsible for their behavior, but with empathy and connection. When you can empathize with your child (by acknowledging their feelings—even if you don't agree), you're then able to connect and redirect your child to choose more appropriate behavior. However, your ability to redirect can only happen once you and your child have calmed down. You've probably experienced this with your own child when you tried to talk with them while they were still in an emotionally reactive state. You also may be able to recall an incident in which you were in an overwhelmed emotional state and a partner, friend, or colleague tried to talk with you about your behavior. Timing is everything. Remember that as humans, we are wired for connection. We also have an innate need to be seen and heard. It's only after this occurs that we're able to self-reflect.

Redirection is possible once your child is ready—once they're able to hear you. As we've already discussed, behavior occurs for a reason. And it's usually because your child is not able to handle their big feelings. So before attempting to talk with your child, ask yourself if they're ready—are they calm enough to hear you? If not, wait. Their behavior doesn't have to be addressed immediately. Let your child know that it needs to be addressed, but not until you're both able to calmly listen and talk. When you're ready to talk, remember to first connect and redirect.

What's the Consequence?

If your main focus when disciplining your child is on what consequence to give, you're missing the point. There's a good chance you're chasing after their behavior, gearing up to give the next consequence when they "mis"behave. You may also be confused as to what consequence to give. Today's "perfect" consequence may not work tomorrow, especially if it's not related to your child's behavior or is punitive in nature. Parents spend a lot of their energy searching for the perfect consequence for their child. Or perhaps they're trying to make sure their child learns a lesson, so they immediately give their child a consequence before actually considering the ramifications—and it's often done in anger. *You're grounded for a month!* (Seriously—a month?) Some parents feel the need to lecture their child. Kids in my practice tell me they'd much prefer a consequence over a lecture simply because the consequence is often shorter than their parent's lengthy lecture. By the time parents consult with me, they've resigned themselves to the fact that consequences don't work for their child. Many parents tell me, "It doesn't matter what I take away; they just don't care. If anything, I pay the price because their behavior only worsens." Consequences have the power to alter a child's behavior, but it really depends on the consequence and how it's delivered.

Consequences are important and necessary. Life is full of consequences. We learn from consequences. If you drive twenty miles over the speed limit, it's likely you'll receive a speeding ticket. If you talk behind a friend's back, you could lose their friendship.

I'd like to make a distinction between consequences and punishment; they are not the same. And it's the blurred line between the two that often trips parents up. What parents believe to be a consequence is often a punishment. A consequence that is not connected to the actual transgression and does not serve to teach the child is a punishment. Telling your teen they cannot go to a party because they didn't do the dishes is a punishment, whereas telling them they can go to a friend's house once the dishes are done is a natural consequence.

There are natural consequences for everything we do in life—and your kids are not immune to them. The term often stumps parents; it's not always easy to discern what a natural consequence might be. I promise you that life provides natural consequences in all situations—they may not be obvious at first, but a consequence will eventually occur. Some parents seem to struggle with allowing their child to experience life's consequences. Because of their own anxiety, they want to protect their child from consequences. Allowing your child to experience life's consequences takes courage—and a willingness to calm your own parental anxiety. Are you willing to let your child experience the consequences of his or her actions?

As parents, it's important we discern when we're able to do this and when we're not. We're not going to let them play with a sharp knife just to learn that knives cause serious injuries. However, can we let go of our parenting grip and allow our child to refuse to do their homework so that they experience the consequence given by their teacher? Although your child's safety is important, are you able to let them take risks in life? Their training wheels on their bike, designed to keep them safe while learning to ride their bike, will only hold them back if kept on too long. Can you allow yourself to feel the fear of letting your child take appropriate risks all the while knowing that they may suffer in the process? A teen who is unable to attend their senior prom because they were caught drinking alcohol during class will learn a valuable lesson from this experience—if the parent does not try to intervene. I've worked with parents who had a difficult time allowing their teen to experience life's consequences. The parents struggled because they didn't want to see their teen suffer. I remind them that their kids suffer more in the long term when they are not given the opportunity to experience consequences.

So before you try to stop or control your child's behavior, teach them to process potential outcomes. Engage them in a conversation. Ask them what might happen if they continue their behavior. And then let them choose their actions for themselves and experience the consequences of their decision. Once you learn to calm your own anxiety and allow your child to take responsibility for their own behavior, you'll witness growth—your child's and your own.

Remember, if you allow it, consequences occur naturally. An unrelated consequence you create is not natural and typically does not teach your child. What children often learn from an arbitrary consequence imposed by their parent is to become more resentful and/or to hide their behavior from you. Chances are your consequences make no sense to your child. What does hitting their sister have to do with not being able to play their video game? Children become resistant and resentful if they do not understand the connection between their behavior and the consequence. They also tend to focus more on your behavior than their own: "My mother is nuts . . . she thinks that taking the car away for a month is going to teach me not to talk back? I'll say whatever I feel like saying!"

As long as your child focuses on you and the consequence you imposed, they will have no reason to focus on themselves. And rescuing them from their own actions by not allowing them to experience consequences outside of your home only teaches them to not take responsibility for their actions. Give your child choices and consequences for the choice they make. In my ScreamFree Parenting classes, we talk about letting "the consequences do the screaming."[46]

Remind yourself to take some time off and calm down before you give a consequence. Appropriate consequences should be created only with a clear, calm mind—not in the heat of the moment. And it's perfectly okay to wait before giving a consequence—sometimes even up to a day (especially with older kids). If possible, try to connect the consequence with the behavior. And don't forget to deliver consequences with empathy—"I understand you're disappointed you can't go away for the weekend. You chose not to start your quarterly research paper before now, so you'll need to do it over the weekend."

As you discipline your child, remind yourself: perfect parenting is not the goal. Neither is raising perfect kids. There will be days when you've think you've mastered this parenting thing, and there will be days when your kids knock you from your parenting pedestal and remind you that you're human. And when that happens, pause, take a few breaths, and reconnect with yourself. Ask yourself once again what your goals are as a parent. Admit when you're wrong and celebrate when you get it right—your kids will appreciate your humility. Discipline takes practice. It's best to practice it when you and your child are calm, not in the heat of the moment. Practice connection and limit-setting on a daily basis rather than waiting until you're frustrated and angry.

Begin to look beyond your child's behavior rather than focusing on behavioral strategies to fix it. Focus on viewing behavioral issues as an opportunity for growth, both your child's and your own. Use these opportunities as teaching tools. Allow your child the freedom to make mistakes and to learn from them. Don't we all want to be given a second chance—a chance to get it right? Your child will appreciate your willingness to give them a chance to try again. That is how they learn. Kids live moment to moment, and most are willing to give parents a second chance—something we as parents can learn. And don't forget to nurture your relationship with your child; their behavior will improve as a result.

Journaling Exercises

- How would you define a consequence? How has your view of consequences changed since you've become a parent?

- As a child, how did you experience consequences? Did your parents use them as a teaching tool or more as a form of punishment?

- Did consequences that were more punitive in nature encourage or discourage you to make changes in your behavior?

- How do you use consequences with your children?

- Do you find your consequences to be effective? If not, why?

- What consequences have you found to be most effective? How did they help your child learn?

- What consequences have been less effective or detrimental to your child's learning or behavior?

- How might you change your children's consequences so that they serve to teach, rather than punish, your child?

- Knowing what I know now, I intend to . . .

Chapter 9

Just Tell Me the Truth

Honesty is more than not lying. It is
truth telling, truth speaking, truth
living, and truth loving.

—James E. Faust

*m*arta, a mother of three, sat in my office and spoke softly about her ten-year-old daughter and fifteen-year-old twin sons, voicing her concern. She appeared to be confident in her mothering ability yet struggled with her kids' unwillingness or inability to tell the truth. She explained, "Sometimes I feel like I'm raising pathological liars, and it scares me." She went on to say, "They've become very good at looking me straight in the eyes while bold-face lying." I assured Marta that I had heard similar stories from parents and, in my many years of practice, had never seen or diagnosed kids as pathological liars. Kids lie—and so do adults. Often, parents plead with their children to tell them the truth, but are they really ready to hear the truth?

Chapter Summary

Children learn to lie as a part of their developmental process, but they also learn by watching the examples of others—particularly their parents. If we allow ourselves to tell white lies, harbor family secrets, or deny our own personal truth, our children witness and mimic those behaviors. However, you can break the cycle for your family by creating a safe, accepting space for truth-telling—ultimately, the truth that will set you and your children free.

Learning the Lie

Let's first examine why kids lie—and they all do. Lying is a normal phenomenon in children. In a child's mind, they're telling their version of the truth (albeit distorted). They do this for two primary reasons—to avoid punishment and to avoid disappointing you. Although lying serves these two primary purposes, kids also lie in order to gain power or a sense of control. And once they learn they're able to fool parents and friends, they're likely to lie again. Chances are you've lied to someone for the very same reasons. Perhaps you didn't want to face the consequences and lied to avoid disappointing someone or have them think less of you. We've all lied at some point in our life—most likely more times than we'd care to admit. So why do parents get so upset with kids when they lie? When you can step back and see your kid's lies for what they are, dropping your fear that you might be raising a pathological liar, you're then able to gain a clearer understanding of what truth hides beneath your kid's lies.

If you're concerned about your child's lying, here is some good news. According to Dr. Victoria Talwar, an assistant professor at Montreal's McGill University and a leading expert on children's lying behavior, "lying is related to intelligence."[47] Most children begin to lie between the ages of two and three. In order to lie, the child first must be able to recognize what is true and then manipulate the truth into a more desirable scenario. They must also have the ability to convince others (often parents) of their new "reality." A child that adamantly denies eating a donut while wiping the powdered sugar from their cheek will continue to try to convince their parent of their innocence, especially if they fear punishment. In the parent's eyes, it's obvious that the child is lying, but to the child, their fabricated "truth" serves to lessen their chance of suffering a consequence.

The longer you engage your child in a seemingly fruitless debate over lying, the deeper they'll dig their heels in—and continue to lie. The story they've created will begin to take on a life of its own. The more detailed the story, the more you just might begin to believe it. Your child's creative imagination might even impress you if you weren't so determined to get to the truth! And your child's story will grow in an effort to keep their "truth" going, all in the hope that you'll finally believe them or give up trying. Their success in convincing you or wearing you down will only serve to fuel their future efforts to lie—as will your inability to hear the real truth. The cycle of lying and punishing will serve only to perpetuate this cycle.

Most parents have little patience for lying and are quick to punish their child for doing so—often by yelling, lecturing, taking away toys, spanking, or shaming their child. I've even seen multiple videos online portraying kids wearing sandwich boards inscribed with the words *I am a liar*. Most likely, the parents who posted these videos had reached the end of their parenting rope. Their anger and frustration surrounding their child's lying prompted them to publicly shame their child. Although I don't condone lying, no child deserves this.

I'd like you to ask yourself how you react when your child tells you an unpleasant truth. Do you react quickly out of frustration and anger, or are you able to calm yourself down before you respond? Based on your typical reaction, do you believe your child is more or less inclined to tell you the truth in the future? Do you encourage or discourage your child to tell the truth? Kids may not know how you'll react to their lies, but they're often more afraid of your reaction if they tell you the truth. At least by lying, they take a chance that they may never have to tell you the truth—and hope you'll never figure out they're lying.

Although your child's lying is normal, it shouldn't be ignored. Lying can become habitual. Those small white lies morph into bigger lies. And each "successful" lie (when they didn't get caught) prompts your child to lie again. Although you want to teach your child to tell the truth, punishing your child for lying will likely encourage them to lie even more. Remember, most times they're lying to avoid punishment. Nevertheless, there are some important steps that you can take to help your child learn to tell the truth.

- ⚘ Be aware of how you react to your child's behavior—are you quick to react with anger and punishment?
  - If so, your reaction will reinforce the likelihood that your child will lie in the future.
  - Instead, learn to calm yourself first and then respond to their behavior; set limits and enforce consequences when necessary.
- ⚘ Don't set your child up to lie by asking them a question if you already know the answer.
  - When you ask your child if they brushed their teeth (after you've checked their toothbrush and it's bone dry), chances are they're going to try with all their might to convince you otherwise.

- Instead, let your child know that you know they didn't brush their teeth and now it's time to do so.

- Give your child a second chance—a chance to get it right.
  - If you can't offer a second chance, ask them what they might do differently next time.
  - Use the situation as a teaching opportunity.

- Accept that your child will make mistakes and may lie to cover them up.
  - Your unconditional love and acceptance of your child will help them begin to accept responsibility for their mistakes and to learn from them. They will be less likely to lie or cover up their mistakes if they know they won't be judged for them.

Remember: your child is watching you every day. They're watching not only to see how you handle their lies but also how you handle your own. Keep in mind that you teach your child to lie when you lie. When you stretch the truth or tell a little white lie, you teach them to lie. When your child hears you tell a coworker or relative over the phone that you're not able to attend a party because you'll be out of town when clearly you have no travel plans, they learn it's okay to lie. Even when you lie to your sibling to avoid conflict and then justify your own behavior to your child by saying *I just don't want to hurt their feelings*, you teach your child to lie. When you're willing to write a note to your child's teacher saying your child didn't finish their homework assignment because they weren't feeling well (even though you know this not to be true), you teach your child to lie. You might not be telling them to lie, but you're still showing them how to lie. After a while, lying becomes a learned behavior and a way to avoid conflict. Those small white lies lead to bigger lies—which are often rationalized and justified.

Before you blame and shame your child about lying, perhaps take a look at your own truths (or lies) and ask yourself if they've become your default mode for handling uncomfortable situations or avoiding conflict in your life. Research reveals disturbing news—the reason children lie is that parents teach them to. According to Dr. Talwar, they learn it from us: "We don't explicitly tell them to lie, but they see us do it. They see us tell the telemarketer, 'I'm just a guest here.' They see us boast and lie to smooth social relationships."[48]

When you become more aware of your own ability to lie, you're also reminded of your responsibility to model truth and integrity for your kids. You have an opportunity to create a safe environment for your children in which they can learn to tell the truth, an environment that encourages them to admit their mistakes and learn from them. You ultimately have the opportunity to create a family culture of *truth-telling*. The world is inundated with people who lie—it seems to be rampant in our society and culturally accepted. What do you want to teach and model for your children? They are watching, and it's your responsibility to teach the virtue of *truth-telling*.

You want your child to tell the truth, but when you say "Just tell me the truth," do you really mean it? Are you ready to hear it, no matter what the truth is? Again, remind yourself that when you react or take what they say personally, you're encouraging or teaching them to lie. After all, why would they want to tell you the truth if they know they're going to have to endure your lecture, rant, or anger? Susan Stiffelman, a practicing psychotherapist, marriage and family therapist, and author of *Parenting Without Power Struggles*, suggests that you:

- Make it safe for your child to tell you the truth.
  - Does your reaction encourage or discourage truth-telling?
  - Be curious about your child's behavior. Try to discern why they failed to turn in an assignment—did they not do it or perhaps lose it?
  - Help your child learn from their mistakes. Ask them what they need or what they might do differently next time.

- Acknowledge your own errors and take responsibility for your own behavior.
  - Remember that your child is watching how you handle your own mistakes.
  - Do you blame others or take responsibility for yourself?
  - Are you defensive about your own behavior?
  - When your child sees you defend your own behavior while placing blame on someone else's, they learn to do the same.
- Address the source of chronic lying.
  - Perhaps your daughter frequently forgets to do her math homework because she is struggling in math. It's easier to use this excuse than to have to face the fact that she doesn't understand her assignment—which triggers her underlying belief that she's stupid.
  - Your firstborn may repeatedly react to his little sister's annoying behavior by throwing her favorite stuffed animal down the stairs. You may be quick to react and admonish him for his behavior, but if this seems to be a chronic issue, be willing to dig a little deeper into their behavior— his sister just might be the instigator![49]

You may not be ready to hear the truth. Your child's truth may not be easy to accept. However, when you're open and are able to welcome all truth in your home, you gift your child with the ability to show up as they are—with honesty. They're able to trust you as their parent because they know you'll accept them fully for who they are, in spite of their mistakes.

Journaling Exercises:

- How do you feel when your child lies to you—any type of lie, small or big?

> What triggers your emotional reactivity when you know they're lying? How do you react? Or do you respond in a calm manner?

> Do you believe your reaction or response encourages or discourages your child to tell the truth? If so, how?

> Do your give your child a second chance?

> List three ways you could respond that would encourage your child to tell the truth.

The Hurt of Protective Lies

Your child needs to be able to trust that you're telling the truth. Kids need to feel safe with their parents and trust that they're speaking the truth. Yet sometimes you may feel the need to lie to your child—in an effort to shelter and protect them. This is usually a result of your own parental anxiety. In an attempt to keep your child from getting hurt, you lie to them, which only results in more hurt. I've worked with children whose parent has died from cancer or a car accident. Often in an effort to help their child feel safe, the surviving parent tries to reassure the child by telling them everything is fine—when all evidence points to the fact that everything is *not* fine. The family may be forced to move out of their home. Reality has set in that dad is not coming back or mom is immobilized by her grief. Pretending everything is fine when it's clearly not actually makes it harder for the child. I recognize, however, that sometimes parents with the best intentions withhold information from their kids in the hope that everything will be fine.

I worked with a six-year-old little girl who was very aware her parents were in trouble—she just wasn't sure what kind of trouble. Although they had not let her in on their plan to divorce, wanting to keep it a secret until she finished the school year, this little girl was very aware of the tension in the family—not because of her parents' outwardly expressed anger (they never argued) but because of the deafening silence between the two. No longer did the family engage in fun activities. Rarely did they spend any time together as a family. Her dad seemed to work all the time, and her mother always complained about being too tired to do anything. Every time this little girl asked her mom what was wrong, her mother quickly replied, *Nothing is wrong—everything is fine.*

This wise little girl didn't buy into her mother's altered truth. What she did do, however, was watch her mother like a hawk, trying to ensure that her mom would be okay. She also began to imagine the worst. Was her mom always tired because she was really sick? Was she going to die? Did her dad have to work all the time because they were running out of money? Had she done something wrong that caused her parents' distress? Some of her unspoken concerns began to surface in her therapy sessions.

I encouraged the parents to tell her as much truth as they thought she could handle while not falsely reassuring her that everything was fine. Initially, they told her that they were having a difficult time in their marriage and they hoped that everything would work out for the best. They actually did begin marriage counseling (something they'd previously resisted). Although they ultimately divorced, their daughter was better prepared than she would have been had they continued to pretend that everything was fine.

In an effort to calm their own anxiety, parents often lie to their children. A diagnosis of cancer is frightening enough for an adult, and they can't imagine burdening their child with this. So rather than being honest about the diagnosis and impending treatment, some parents avoid telling the truth. Again, children are left to wonder, and their imagination creates scenarios that are far worse than reality.

Children often know the truth, but because their parents lie to them, the child not only learns to distrust their parents—they also learn to distrust themselves. According to Kate Roberts, PhD, author of *Savvy Parenting*, "Researchers at MIT have found that children are not gullible and they can in fact sense when parents are lying to them, causing them to distrust the very people who are their caretakers. Children also know when parents are withholding information."[50]

Providing false reassurance does not reassure your child. They learn to doubt their own intuition and stop trusting themselves—and that is never a good thing. Your kids can handle just about any truth when they know you're there to help them process and handle it. And your child will be able to handle the truth only as well as you're able.

The Truth about Family Secrets

Some families keep secrets and work tirelessly to keep them hidden. Family secrets are created out of shame—embarrassment about someone's behavior in the family. Whether it's a job loss, a failing marriage, or alcoholism, whenever there is shame, secrets are created to protect individuals or the family as a whole. Family secrets are often passed down from generation to generation.[51] These secrets unite or divide family members. And when there are secrets in the family, children learn unhealthy communication patterns. Secrets can create miscommunication or complete emotional or physical cut-off in families. Family members take sides, divide, or become completely estranged from one another.

Although kids may not know the secrets, they are sent messages about what's okay to talk about and what is not. Kids also take on the shame of the family. When you withhold important family information from your child, you do them a disservice. Although a child may not be privy to hidden information or secrets, they often know when something is amiss in the family. Our families are our first relationships, and we learn from each relationship. Many healthy lessons can be learned from our family of origin when truth is spoken, just as unhealthy lessons are learned when it is not.

A mother who gave birth to a baby boy reminisced about her first infant son whom she gave up for adoption when she was a young teen. Although she had wanted to keep the baby, she was not equipped emotionally or financially to be a mom at that time. A private adoption was handled through her church, and she never had any further contact with the baby or the adoptive parents. She grieved at the time but then went on with her life.

Flash forward: the mother was happily married and looked forward to the birth of her baby. Although she had vivid memories of her first pregnancy years ago, the impact of the birth of her newly born son was not something she anticipated. At times, she found herself comparing her two infants—their similarities and differences. Although she felt a bond with her new son, she began to quietly long for the infant she had let go. This became most apparent when each year around the time of the anniversary of the adoption, the mom became very sad.

She never spoke to her son about the baby, but he sensed something was wrong. He was also very aware that each November, a few days before Thanksgiving, his mom spent most of her time in her room. Sometimes he'd see her cry, asking if anything was wrong. She always replied, "No, I'm fine." This pattern continued for years. As he became a young man, he described his relationship with his mom as "distant." He expressed that although he worked hard to earn her love, sometimes he felt he just couldn't reach her. She didn't show much affection for him and even seemed sad around his birthday. Years later, he discovered that he had not been her first son. He didn't learn this from his mother but from a relative. In some ways, it was a relief to him to know why his mother had been distant, but he also suffered his own loss—the loss of his mother's love.

I've worked with many adopted children. Some adoptive parents were forthcoming and allowed their child to know about the adoption, whereas others were not—in a loving attempt to "protect" their child. To protect them from the possibility of feeling abandoned—not loved or wanted. Kids usually discover the truth. And when the family chose to keep the adoption secret, more damage was done to the child. The message the child received was that there was something wrong about being adopted; therefore, the family needed to create a secret.

Family secrets damage relationships.[52] They also have the ability to shatter a child's world, even into adulthood. Their reality is no longer real. There are many parents who delay getting divorced until their kids are grown. I've worked with many moms who continue to struggle with their parents' divorce. The belief that they've held onto is that their childhood was a lie—the "happy" family was a sham. I've also worked with mothers who've carried the burden of a family secret, internalizing the stress and anxiety. They've subsequently developed physical and emotional debilitating conditions—ones that seem to have no clinical diagnosis or treatment. Normal childhood development may be delayed or arrested depending upon the trauma associated with the family secret. Family secrets can affect a child's emotional growth, self-worth, and identity. It's not until they're able to release the family secret and emotional undercurrent that healing may begin.

Children always fare better when they know the truth. As I've discussed before, they don't need to know every detail, but trust that if you don't offer some truth, there is a good chance they'll create a truth far worse than the actual truth.

Family secrets that are passed from generation to generation lead to more family heartache and dysfunction. What you learn in your family of origin is unconsciously repeated in your current family—unless you choose differently. You have an opportunity to break the cycle of family secrets. I know, personally, the value of doing so.

My family of origin kept secrets. My dad suffered from alcoholism, and my mom did everything in her power to keep it a secret—enabling his behavior in the process. My dad rarely faced the consequences because my mom quickly picked up the messy pieces along the way. In an effort to keep others from finding out, my mother made excuses for him. She managed his business in every way possible to keep his secret. As children, we were told (actually threatened) to never speak about it outside the house. In fact, it was rarely talked about in the privacy of our home. And so we too learned to keep the family secret. I discovered years later that close family friends, living next to us and across the street, had no idea what was going on behind our closed doors. They were shocked to discover my dad's alcoholism. Our family friends were very helpful and caring, and had they known, they could have been a wonderful support.

While family secrets might initially unite families, they have the power to destroy. *Truth-telling* has the power to heal, depending upon the timing and delivery. If you've been a keeper of family secrets, I urge you to seek help for yourself and your family. It is helpful to work with a family therapist who specializes in familial relationships. They will be there to support you in uncovering the hidden secrets and ending your role as the keeper of family secrets. If you decide to reveal a family secret, you'll be gifted with the chance to heal yourself and your children.

> Give a child an unpalatable truth and she will figure out a way to process it. But "protect" her and the ghosts will whisper in her ear.
>
> —*Meg Rosoff*

Journaling Exercises

Are you aware of any family secrets in your family of origin? How long have you known the secrets? How did you find out about them?

- Do any other family members know the secrets? If so, who?

- Who are you hiding the secret from? What would it take to reveal the family secret? How might your life change if you did reveal the secret?

- Are you keeping family secrets from your children? If so, why? Do you think they're aware of any secrets?

- What could you do to break the cycle of secrets in your family?

Can You Tell Yourself the Truth?

It takes courage to speak the truth. It also takes great courage to speak your own *real truth*—first to yourself and then to others. Many women bypass their truth, believing it's too painful to look at. We all fear being vulnerable and exposed. I think we can all relate to fears of vulnerability. Brené Brown describes vulnerability in this manner: "Vulnerability sounds like truth and feels like courage. Truth and courage aren't always comfortable, but they're never weakness."[53]

Hiding from the truth may be easier, in the short term. However, your willingness and courage to be open to the truth may grant you a lifetime of freedom—freedom to speak your truth and show up fully, as you are. And your willingness to show up authentically, with all of your shining gifts and imperfections, will allow others to do the same. Your ability to be authentic depends on your ability to face your truth. Denying your truth is a form of betrayal—a betrayal of yourself. How long have you been showing the world only a piece of yourself? Perhaps your best piece? Or maybe you've not allowed yourself to shine in front of others—making yourself less than in an effort to make others feel better. The mask you wear (yes, we all do) serves only to hide your true essence. Your whole self—both your gifts and your faults. When you allow yourself to be fully human, complete with beautiful gifts and flaws, you give yourself permission to be real.

I'm reminded of the beauty of being "real" each time I read this quote from *The Velveteen Rabbit*:

> "Real isn't how you are made," said the Skin Horse. "It's a thing that happens to you. When a child loves you for a long, long time, not just to play with, but REALLY loves you, then you become Real."
>
> "Does it hurt?" asked the Rabbit.
>
> "Sometimes," said the Skin Horse, for he was always truthful. "When you are Real you don't mind being hurt."
>
> "Does it happen all at once, like being wound up," he asked, "or bit by bit?"

"It doesn't happen all at once," said the Skin Horse. "You become. It takes a long time. That's why it doesn't happen often to people who break easily, or have sharp edges, or who have to be carefully kept. Generally, by the time you are Real, most of your hair has been loved off, and your eyes drop out, and you get loose in the joints and very shabby. But these things don't matter at all, because once you are Real you can't be ugly, except to people who don't understand."[54]

You've probably spent time with people who seem "perfect." You've secretly wondered how they're able to pull perfection off while making it look so easy. Most likely, they're working very hard at it. And chances are they're also working very hard to hide aspects of themselves that they don't want the world to see. I know this to be true because I used to be that person.

Perfection is what I strived for in my childhood and continued to carry into my adult life. I now work very hard to allow *all* of myself to show, to let my full self be seen—all aspects of me. And it is very freeing. Maybe this happens with experience and age. From one woman to another (yes, a bit older than you): show your whole self sooner than later. I promise you everything will be okay. And if you lose some friends in the process, they weren't your real tribe. Your real tribe is there to support you however you show up!

It's always helpful to remember that when perfectionism is driving, shame is riding shotgun.

—*Brené Brown*, Rising Strong

A few years ago, I attended a women's retreat. We did an activity that encouraged us to take a closer look ourselves—the inner and outer. We used paper masks and were instructed to write down the characteristics that we like to share with the world on the outside of the mask. That was the easy part. As I began to self-reflect, I noticed many women were sharing their characteristics with each other as they wrote them on the front of the mask. I realized it didn't take me long and was fairly easy to identify my outer words—friendly, kind, compassionate, loving, and sensitive.

We were then instructed to turn to the inside of the mask and identify our inner self, the one we hide from the world—our shadow side. I hesitated, as did most of the women, before I wrote these words—jealous, judgmental, and angry. I found myself holding my breath as I looked at the words. *Could these really be me?* Angry was certainly something I worked very hard to avoid being in my life—I grew up in an angry family and worked very hard to avoid it in my own family. Anger was certainly not something I was comfortable with or welcomed in my current family.

As I sat there staring at my inner words, I took some deep breaths and my heart began to soften. The facilitator reminded of us of the importance of identifying and accepting our shadow side (our imperfections). We learned that we all have imperfections, and when we learn to embrace them, we're able to show up as our whole self. No longer do we feel the need to hide our imperfections. I felt myself breathing softly again as I contemplated how much easier life would be if I allowed myself to accept everything about me. I realized that even in accepting my shadow, I didn't have to act from that place—I had a choice. Simply by acknowledging my imperfections, I didn't have to hide from them. I now had a choice: I could show up with jealousy and resentment, or I could acknowledge my feelings and choose to take on a new perspective—under any circumstance.

After studying my mask, both the inner and outer, I felt good about myself. I'd walked through my vulnerability with courage—and found a new sense of freedom. Exposing my shadow to myself and others reminded me that I didn't have to hide behind it anymore. However, our last assignment put me to the test. We partnered with one another and shared our inner and outer masks. I actually welcomed sharing my mask, but I had a different experience than the one I'd anticipated.

We were instructed to listen to our partner describe their characteristics, be supportive, and not judge. As I sat facing my partner (whom I didn't know), I first shared my outer mask (the easier one to share, of course!). She smiled and affirmed my positive qualities. I then offered my inner mask. Her reaction was priceless. She backed her chair away from me and said, "Ew. If I had those characteristics, I would not be sharing them with the world. Those are awful!" I took a breath and began to laugh. Not a nervous laugh, but one of relief. I thought to myself, *Well, I was just given an opportunity to experience what normally would have felt like criticism and judgment—something that often stopped me in my tracks—yet I am still okay!*

Actually, I was more than okay because I knew I was still a good person. I no longer needed to hide this inner aspect from myself or others. I also realized that because I'd fully accepted and loved myself for all my gifts and imperfections, I would always be okay. I no longer needed to depend on others to validate my own goodness. My experience with the retreat partner was a wonderful gift, and I was grateful! My belief that "life happens *for you*, not *to you*" was reconfirmed that day.

> Because true belonging only happens when we present our authentic, imperfect selves to the world, our sense of belonging can never be greater than our level of self-acceptance.
>
> —*Brené Brown*, Daring Greatly

Journaling Exercises

Take some time to complete the Journaling Exercises and remind yourself: your ability to speak your own truth first will free you to speak your truth to others.

- How do you portray yourself to others? What truth do you tell the world?

- What truth do you tell yourself?

- ✥ List five characteristics about yourself that you believe are positive.

- ✥ What are some ways you share these characteristics with people in your life?

- ✥ List five characteristics about yourself that you deem to be more negative.

- ✥ How do these show up in your life?

- ✥ How easy is it for you to acknowledge your positive characteristics?

- ✥ How easy or difficult is it for you to acknowledge your negative qualities?

- ✥ How might your life change if you were courageous enough to explore your shadow—your imperfections?

The opposite of recognizing that we're feeling something is denying our emotions. The opposite of being curious is disengaging. When we deny our stories and disengage from tough emotions, they don't go away; instead, they own us, they define us. Our job is not to deny the story, but to defy the ending—to rise strong, recognize our story, and rumble with the truth until we get to a place where we think, *Yes. This is what happened. This is my truth. And I will choose how this story ends.*

—*Brené Brown*

All women and mothers suffer when they don't speak their truth, not only individually but collectively. When a woman minimizes her intellect and abilities in order to help a coworker feel better about herself, she suffers, as do women that follow her. When a mother does not speak the truth about her own eating disorder out of shame for herself and her children, they all suffer. When a mother remains quiet by not speaking her truth about discrimination in her community, the mother, her children, and her community suffer.

Truth-telling takes courage—and it's hard.

But what is even harder is remaining silent with yourself and others. Sitting in silence in order to not make waves does not serve anyone. Showing up by telling the truth is empowering and liberating. But first, you have to be willing to speak your own truth.

Sometimes, women will do just about anything to avoid being truthful. You may relate to this. If you find yourself justifying your dishonesty, know that you're lying to yourself—and ultimately betraying yourself. Although you may rationalize your behavior, you're being dishonest. And according to Jonathan Wells, life coach and author of the blog post "Do You Have the Courage to Be Honest?," you're doing this to avoid pain—pain related to:

- Trying to spare someone's feelings or pride.
- Not wanting others to think badly of you.
- Being afraid that someone might steal your recognition.
- Thinking that you are protecting someone.
- Protecting your ego by avoiding embarrassment.
- Making an effort to help others save face.
- Feeling threatened that your image or reputation is on the line.
- Disliking someone but not wanting them to know.[55]

Integrity is telling myself the truth. And
honesty is telling the truth to other people.

—*Spencer Johnson*

Facing your truth is a courageous act and, ultimately, freeing.
Often, we cling to our distorted truths. We tell ourselves that things
will get better when evidence shows us otherwise. We often delay
looking at our truth in the hope that what we avoid seeing will go
away. An alcoholic may convince themselves that they don't have a
problem and are able to drink just one drink—and then they have
three. Our ego tries to protect us from facing the truth. I have worked
with several single mothers who retrospectively knew their marriage
was falling apart, but it was too painful to look at. So they pretended
that everything was okay—until it wasn't.

We ignore the truth of the pain. We avoid it at all costs and even
try to numb the pain with alcohol, drugs, and other addictions such
as food, work, and shopping—the list goes on and on. We busy ourselves, our lives, all in an effort to avoid feeling what we are feeling.

Owning our story and loving ourselves
through that process is the bravest thing
we'll ever do.

—*Brené Brown*

Chances are you've spent a lot of energy avoiding your own emotional pain. And in the process, you've actually told false stories about
yourself—to yourself and others. Before you're able to seek your
truth, it's important to examine what you've been telling yourself. Just
as your child has learned to lie, so have you—ever since you were a
child. What lies have you been telling others and, more importantly,
yourself? Do any of these common lies noted by Farnoosh Brock resonate with you?

- Lie #1: You are not worthy of love.
- Lie #2: You are not enough.
- Lie #3: You do not deserve happiness.
- Lie #4: You are not unique or special.
- Lie #5: Your dreams are too unrealistic or impractical.
- Lie #6: Your circumstances dictate your success.
- Lie #7: You are not worthy of wealth.[56]

Telling yourself these lies does not serve you or your children. Your thoughts about yourself become your belief. Glennon Doyle Melton, founder of *Momastery*, encourages truth-telling and hope-spreading. Her social movement has encouraged mothers to speak their truth. She has built a supportive community for moms, a community that reminds moms that they're not alone. I applaud her for her heart and efforts. She's given moms permission to celebrate their imperfections, to no longer hide behind perfectionism. She urges moms to show up fully, even if they feel they're not ready. She says, "I don't have anything figured out, and you know what? I'm showing up anyway, and amazing things are happening. And that's what people do who change the world; they just show up before they're ready."[57]

> Courage starts with showing up and letting ourselves be seen.
>
> —*Brené Brown*, Daring Greatly

How will you know what it feels like to show up if you don't show up? You won't know until you do, even if you don't feel ready. How will you know you're ready, anyway? You won't. Even if you work hard to get ready—by losing weight, learning a new skill, or making sure you're perfect (whatever that means)—you probably won't feel ready. The only way you'll know what it's like to show up is to go ahead and show up! And as the saying goes, "When in doubt, fake it till you make it!"

It takes courage to show up. Living life fully is not for wimps or for the faint of heart—it's for the brave ones who choose not to sit back in fear. When will you feel completely safe? What will it take? And chances are, if you're waiting until you feel safe, you're missing out on a whole lot of life. Marie Kondo, author of *The Life-Changing Magic of Tidying Up*, states, "People cannot change their habits without first changing their way of thinking." She goes on to say, "Even if they're initially inspired, they can't stay motivated and their efforts peter out. The root cause lies in the fact that they can't see the results or feel the effects."[58] This applies not only to tidying up your house and your health habits but also to your thoughts and the stories you create. If you can't feel the overwhelmingly positive effect of a clean, organized house (if that gives you joy) or celebrate your success in losing the ten pounds you'd promised yourself you'd lose, then why bother? If your efforts are not sustained by a feeling of success (because you gave up after a few days), then why would you continue?

This also applies to changing your thoughts and stories—and having the willingness and courage to show up—again and again, in spite of how you believe the world sees you. If I never allowed myself to show my imperfections (my shadow jealousy, judgement, and anger) after I was shamed by my partner at the women's retreat, I too would have missed out on all the gifts I've received from those who accept me fully for who I am. As you learn to show up again and again, without self-judgment, you too will be given gifts. And don't forget: you are enough—you are *more than enough*.

I have one final word of wisdom: Your truth should be shared—but not necessarily with everyone. Not all friends and acquaintances deserve to hear your truth. Your truth may not be safe with them. This is where your ability to discern whom you can trust your truth with really matters. Have you ever been brave enough to share something with a friend, and after telling them, they belittle you—or share your story with someone else without your permission? Truth-telling should only be shared with those you trust. Brené Brown states, "If we can share our story with someone who responds with empathy and understanding, shame can't survive." [59]

When we model truth-telling both to ourselves and to the world, our children witness and are changed by this. Their honesty is learned from ours. Teach them the value of integrity and show them the meaning in your own conversation and interactions. Show up fully, and your children will trust you with their truth, too.

Journaling Exercises

- Are you showing up or waiting until you're ready? How will you know you're ready?

- How would your life change for the better if you just decided to show up—ready or not? What's stopping you?

- Ready, set—just show up! Be brave! And journal here about your awesome braveness.

- Knowing what I know now, I intend to . . .

Chapter 10

Clearing Your Past So You Can Parent in the Present

The greatest burden a child must bear is
the unlived life of the parents.

—Carl Jung

A parent's state of mind and emotional well-being has a significant impact on their children. Children who choose to become parents will influence their own children—and the cycle continues. Parents bearing emotional scars (and we all do) often unintentionally pass along the burdens and wounds to the next generation. The wounds continue to fester and scars are shared until an individual stops, looks the past squarely in the eye, and makes a change within themselves. As a mom, you have the opportunity and ability to terminate (by healing) your own emotional wounding, that which has been passed down to you from previous generations. You alone can be the courageous mother and stop the cycle, for your children and their children. The impact of doing so will help create a vast ripple effect for present and future generations to come, an effect which will help bring peace to your family and the world—and it all begins with you.

> One person can influence their family, one family can influence another, then another, then ten, one hundred, one thousand more, and the whole of humanity will benefit.
>
> —*Tenzin Gyatso, Dalai Lama XIV*

Chapter Summary

Parenting in the present is difficult, particularly when you keep re-experiencing emotions from your past. As children, we all receive messages that influence our emotional well-being. Messages, some healthy, some not, come from our parents and from others too; other adults may unconsciously project their pain onto innocent children. Resurrected, unresolved emotions are detrimental to our ability to parent well, making us more reactive to situations than may be warranted. When we face our repressed emotions, especially those from childhood traumas, we begin the process of healing for ourselves and our family. We free up our personal resources to meet our children's need to grow to be emotionally healthy adults.

When the Past Invades the Present

Maya, a thirty-five-year-old mother of two teens, sat in my office with a distressed expression. "I'm not sure what's wrong—if it's my kids or me." When I asked her to explain what she was feeling, she stated that she felt like she was losing herself and was scared. Although she loved her kids and husband, she felt herself beginning to pull away. She quickly reassured me (or herself) that everything was fine in her marriage. "My husband is very supportive, and a loving husband and father, although he works a lot of hours."

Maya's girls were thirteen and fifteen, were on the honor roll, and played volleyball. Although Maya felt her family was connected, she noticed that her girls were distancing themselves, staying busy with their own pursuits. Maya recognized that their behavior was typical of teens but said their interest in being with their friends more than her still hurt. She tried not to take it personally. The more she tried to engage her daughters in family activities, the more they resisted.

When I asked Maya about her childhood, she told me that she had believed she had a "perfect" childhood with very loving parents and a loving home. That is until her parents announced they were getting divorced. This unexpected news rocked Maya's world. "After all, my parents never even argued," she said. She never heard a disrespectful word between them. But Maya did admit she didn't have many memories of her parents spending time together, since her dad worked very long hours and spent much of his time at home watching TV.

As it turns out, Maya's mother was fed up with holding the family together (as she later told Maya) and felt she had lost herself. Maya painfully remembered the day that her mother announced she was leaving the family for another man—her high school sweetheart. Both Maya and her sister experienced overwhelming feelings of abandonment. As hard as she tried, Maya could not convince her mother to stay. Maya went to great lengths to please her mother, to no avail. She was thirteen when her parents separated. Coincidentally, Maya's youngest daughter was now thirteen. Because of her husband's busy work schedule and her daughters' normal developmental stage of individuating and pulling away from the family, Maya was re-experiencing feelings of abandonment—feelings from childhood buried long ago. She recalled her many attempts to gain her daughters' love and attention, much as she'd done with her mother. Maya offered her daughters enticing invitations for fun outings, which they often declined. Sometimes, she would offer to take her daughters shopping to buy them a new outfit or the latest electronic gadget. This often worked, more frequently than the invitation for family time, until the next time her daughters wanted to go out with their friends.

Maya re-experienced her feelings of abandonment from her mother's rejection with her own husband and daughters. All of us re-live our childhood unconsciously into our adulthood, often replaying the same script over and over again, only with different characters. We repeatedly re-experience feelings we've long since buried (or so we think). Sometimes, these intense feelings left over from our unexamined wounds appear when least expected and stop us in our tracks. And it's often our children that trigger wounds from our childhood. Childhood wounds most likely have created distortions in our thoughts and beliefs—and we act and react from them. And we are not able to effectively meet our children's emotional needs until we're able to meet our own.

Very few people survive childhood without being emotionally wounded, even by seemingly insignificant events like not being invited to a friend's birthday party and feeling left out. But they also can result when a parent is not attuned to their child's needs. Although the child is fed and clothed, emotional needs are not being met. Excessive shaming, neglect, or abuse, cause more severe emotional wounding. Each of the wounds inflicted sends a message that, if left unresolved, impacts how we interact with and perceive the world. A teacher who publically berates a child for being lazy, for example, may be harboring childhood pain. Perhaps they were told they were lazy many years ago. Left unexamined and unresolved, childhood wounds and unhealthy messages are taken unconsciously into adulthood. There, these wounds fester and permeate the person's way of being as an individual and a parent.

Our unexamined wounds have the potential to continue the wound cycle in our newly created family. We actually end up re-creating the very outcome we're hoping to avoid. Whether you parent completely opposite how you were parented or consciously choose the way you wish to parent, you will unconsciously parent from a wounded reactive state when your emotional wounds are activated. In her article "Prepare for Parenting by Healing Your Childhood Wounds," Rita Brhel states, "Even parents who somehow go the very opposite way of how they were parented can go too far. Without addressing their childhood wounds, their internal compass can't orient itself accurately and parents may respond to their children not because they want something better for their child, though they do, but rather out of fear of whatever they are trying to avoid."[60] Once you become more aware of your own inner wounds and demons, you're better able to consciously choose how you want to parent. You begin to have a better understanding of yourself. Your anger that arises when you feel minimized or discounted makes sense because you remember feeling this way as a child. Your fear of speaking your truth as an adult is a reminder of how you felt unheard by your mother or father during childhood.

Unexamined, your unhealed wounds have the ability to re-traumatize you. And they will not only affect you personally, but they also have the propensity to traumatize others. Unexamined wounds affect all of your relationships, especially the ones with your children. Children do not have the skills to cope with your unhealthy emotions. Even the most loving parents are capable of passing down their own emotional baggage to their children, the very wounds that most likely were passed down to them by their own parents. As a mother, you have the power and responsibility to identify your emotional wounds, seek healing, and change your story—for yourself and your children.

Our hidden feelings and internal beliefs ultimately create a distorted veil through which we see the world. Karol K. Truman, author of *Feelings Buried Alive Never Die*, explains, "In our younger years, many of us were taught to shut off or close down the emotional facet of our Be-ing. We were programmed to deny feelings, to bury them. If our feelings were hurt or we didn't like something the way it was, we were taught to 'forget it,' 'ignore it,' 'it doesn't matter,' 'don't think about it,' or 'be quiet and it might go away.'"[61] The truth is, our unresolved feelings never go away—they remain in our psyche. We unconsciously carry our unresolved feelings and emotional baggage into adulthood—where they're played out again and again, often within marriages and certainly with our own children. Many unresolved conflicts in our family of origin are resurrected and reenacted in our current family in one form or another. We also take our buried feelings into our work world, community, and friendships.

The saying "What we resist persists" offers sage advice. Most likely, the unwanted emotions you felt as a child and have worked so hard to ignore and suppress have reared or will rear their ugly head in your relationships with others. Either you'll recognize something in another that triggers your memories or you'll re-create what you experienced during childhood. Most likely, you'll go out of your way to avoid your stuffed emotional baggage. Once hurtful, you've put it away and most likely believe it's in the past—yet you've unconsciously carried this heavy load.

Harville Hendrix, PhD, author of *Getting the Love You Want*, states: "From my observations of thousands of couples . . . I have concluded that it is a compelling need to heal old childhood wounds. The ultimate reason you fell in love with your mate is not that he or she was young and attractive, had an impressive job, had a 'point value' equal to yours, or had a kind disposition. . . . Your old brain believed that it had finally found the ideal candidate to make up for the psychological and emotional damage you experienced in childhood." He further explains, "We cope as well as we can with the world and our relationships by using the feeble set of defenses born of the pain of childhood, a time when parts of our true nature were suppressed in the unconscious. We look grown up—we have jobs and responsibilities—but we are walking wounded, trying desperately to live life fully while unconsciously hoping to somehow restore the sense of joyful aliveness we began with."[62]

Whether you experienced abuse, were parented by a mother who suffered from depression, or experienced the death of a parent during childhood, you were emotionally scarred. Even if you had the most well-meaning parents, your needs were not met 100 percent of the time. Your parents would have had to be superhuman to meet all your needs all the time. Your unmet needs prompted you to develop coping mechanisms to help you regain a sense of security. Your coping mechanisms and defenses may have appeared to have served you during childhood. However, these exact same coping mechanisms are now actually the ones that are potentially hindering your own growth and affecting how you parent your child.

Perhaps you grew up not feeling good enough as a child. In an effort to try to be *good enough*, you tried to be even better, especially in the eyes of your parents. We've all experienced times in our life when we felt weren't measuring up; however, some children raised in dysfunctional families struggle with an unending search to be better. Often, these children are "parentified" in their family and assume the role of parenting their own parent simply because their parent does not have the emotional maturity to nurture the child. These children feel responsible for taking care of their parent while also feeling responsible for their parent's well-being and happiness. According to Karyl McBride, PhD, author of *Will I Ever Be Good Enough?: Healing the Daughters of Narcissistic Mothers*, "Adult children of narcissistic parents commonly grow up with this nagging feeling that they flunked childhood and it's all their fault. They internalize the message they are not good enough no matter how hard they try."[63] Children raised by a narcissistic parent learn early on to please their parent in order to win their love. A parent who is narcissistic is incapable of providing empathy or unconditional love for their children. A child is unable to understand this and, therefore, believes they are unworthy of love. It's often not until early adulthood or even later that their feelings of unworthiness become painfully evident. The cycle continues as a child tries to earn their parent's love while the parent withholds. The child believes, *If my parent doesn't love me, who will?* The narcissistic parent is incapable of acknowledging their own feelings, let alone their child's. So the child's feelings are not heard or validated.

Children of alcoholics also take on the role of trying to change or fix their parent. They fail miserably and as a result take on the message *If I were a better person, this wouldn't be happening. If only I could do better, my parents would stop drinking.*

Out of an endless attempt to feel love from their parent, a child seeks perfection. This endless search is a result of believing that they will be loved once they're perfect. Perfectionism is rooted in shame. Shame of *I'm not lovable because I'm not good enough—not worthy enough.* Children who seek perfection often continue to seek perfection into adulthood.

I worked with Lynn, a mother who was a self-proclaimed perfectionist. Although Lynn was willing to acknowledge these tendencies, she struggled to understand why. She also struggled with the fact that her twelve-year-old daughter seemed to be following in her perfectionistic footsteps. As much as Lynn resisted her own need to ensure perfection in everything she did, she hated to see her daughter do the same. Lynn didn't want her daughter to suffer and carry this burden as she herself continued to do.

When I asked Lynn to reflect on her childhood, she stated that she was the only girl in her family. Her two brothers were four and six years older than she. I asked if there was a time in her life when she felt free to make mistakes. She quickly replied, "Never!" She further explained that she felt loved and rewarded by her mother only when everything was in order and done right. If her handwriting was "sloppy," her mother insisted she rewrite the homework assignment. If Lynn played outside and came home with dirty or ripped clothes, which rarely happened, she was reprimanded. Simply her mother's facial expression alerted Lynn to the fact that her mother was not pleased. There were times that Lynn wondered if her mother even loved her.

Her brothers' relationship with their mom seemed much more relaxed. Lynn stated that if they came home dirty or produced a messy homework assignment, her mother seemed to let it slide—often making the comment "Boys will be boys."

When Lynn was asked to describe her mother, her adjectives painted a picture of a woman who was perfectly groomed, kept a tidy house, and received many community awards for her honor and dedication. Lynn could never remember a time when her mom "let her hair down" and relaxed. She also never remembered a time when her mother made a mistake. In Lynn's eyes, her mother was perfect. Lynn's seemingly *perfect* mother was her first female role model. Not only did Lynn learn to seek perfection in order to feel accepted and loved by her mother, but she also carried her need to please into adulthood.

Children who continuously seek their parents' approval become adults who constantly seek approval of others. I've worked with many moms who have difficulty saying no so as not to disappoint others. They end up saying yes to everything and everyone: yes to projects and committees they have no interest in or time to complete; yes to their boss, even when they know that what they're agreeing to is going to be very difficult to accomplish given the deadline; yes to their parent; yes to their partner; yes to their children—all the while unconsciously screaming, *No, no, no!* Mothers who grew up trying to please their parent continue their efforts to please their own child in an effort to show their child the love that they themselves so desperately wanted or to assure themselves that they will be loved by their child. I've heard many parents admit their own resistance to telling their child no because they want their child to still love them.

Many children raised in dysfunctional families spend most of their childhood feeling guilty, feeling that if they were better, their family would be fine. I once overheard a seven-year-old girl tell her friend, "If I wasn't bad, my family would be fine." I can only imagine how her guilt shadowed her existence during childhood and perhaps into adulthood. Many mothers, even ones who appear to have had the best of childhoods, carry this guilt around. It doesn't go away on its own until you get to the root of it. Feelings of guilt continue to creep in, and mothers feel this insatiable need to say "I'm sorry, so sorry" when they've done nothing wrong. Many women in general have fallen prey to the words *I'm sorry.*

I recently noticed a social media post reporting a movement urging women to purge the words *I'm sorry* from their daily language. The incessant apologies of mothers indicate their underlying assumption that they are the cause of the problem, a message they inherently picked up from childhood—from a variety of sources including parents, family, teachers, and the media.

There are also children who carry feelings of not being "good enough." Rather than striving for perfection, they amplify their abilities in an effort to feel better than others. This becomes their defense mechanism. They boast about their athletic abilities, the number of friends they have, or how much money their parents make. They often become grandiose in their thinking. They're also very quick to defend themselves or blame others. It's too painful for them to believe they are *less than* in any way. Even constructive criticism is too painful for them to hear, so they quickly deflect and project it onto another. They become defensive and are quick to point fingers at others. They have difficulty taking responsibility for themselves. Their late school assignment is not their fault but the fault of their friend who told them the wrong due date. A toy they broke is blamed on their brother, who was coincidentally walking through the room when the toy was thrown. We see similar behavior in adults. You may recognize some of these characteristics in a friend, partner, or yourself.

Ben, a seemingly self-assured eight-year-old boy, came to my office with his mother. I'd met his parents for an initial visit the previous week. Ben's parents expressed concern about his boastful and bossy behavior, especially during playdates. It appeared that Ben needed to feel in charge. He rarely allowed his friends to choose a play activity. Ben was also a "poor sport" according to his mom and dad. If he wasn't winning, he didn't want to play. He'd storm off in the middle of a game. They also noticed that Ben tried to one-up his friends. If a friend proudly announced he'd passed his karate test and earned the next belt, Ben would retort, "Karate is stupid—I play baseball and have five trophies. Baseball is much better than karate!"

Ben's parents' concern that his friends would no longer want to play with him was beginning to happen. Over the past six months, he'd received fewer birthday party and playdate invitations. If Ben extended a playdate invitation to friends, often they were too busy. Although Ben's parents tried to coach Ben on how to be a good friend, he became defensive and blamed his friends.

During my first session with Ben, I asked him about school and friends. He was quick to inform me he was the smartest in his class and had so many friends he couldn't even count them all. I observed the surprised look on his mother's face. I asked Ben to tell me what he was good at (his strengths) and also to explain what he needed help with (his weaknesses). He rattled off many of his strengths, and some appeared a bit grandiose. ("I'm the strongest in my class and can pick up everybody, even my teacher, Mr. Brooks.") Again, his mother sat behind Ben silently shaking her head from side to side.

When it came time to list the things Ben needed help with, he assured me there were none. I offered that we all have things that are hard for us and that we need help with—even adults. Once again, he told me, "I'm good at everything!" His exuberant behavior was above and beyond a dose of healthy self-esteem. I determined my job was to help Ben and his parents understand the source of his need to be *better than*.

Over the next few play therapy sessions with Ben, it became apparent that his small size (he was in the fifth percentile for height on the growth chart) was a contributing factor. In order to feel bigger, he needed to feel better than. Other contributing factors included his diagnosis of ADHD (attention-deficit hyperactivity disorder) and associated learning difficulties. His underlying feelings of being dumb and stupid (overtly expressed to his parents quite often) created a need to feel smarter than. In his attempt to feel better about himself, Ben felt the need to make others feel less than.

Some children experience feelings of not being enough and feel invisible in their family. Their parent's attention, more often than not, is focused on one of the other kids in the family—perhaps the "prettiest," "most talented," or "intellectually gifted" child. Or the attention might be focused on the "difficult" child. The end result is that the other children in the family don't feel seen or heard and therefore feel invisible in the parent's eyes. Those children grow up believing their presence is of no value. As a result, in adulthood, they try to stay hidden, feeling vulnerable and exposed when attention is brought to them. Although these children and adults may just be more introverted, it would be wise to question why. Is their introverted tendency related to their nature or how they were nurtured?

According to Alice Miller, author of *The Drama of the Gifted Child*, "The damage done to us during our childhood cannot be undone, since we cannot change anything in our past. We can, however, change ourselves. We become free by transforming ourselves from unaware victims of the past into responsible individuals in the present, who are aware of our past and are thus able to live with it." She states, "Most people do exactly the opposite. Without realizing that the past is constantly determining their present actions, they avoid learning anything about their history."[64]

Until we're willing to see our past for what it is, we continue to let the past influence our future.

Journaling Exercises

⊛   Do you find yourself getting repeatedly getting stuck in the same story? Do any stories resonate with your childhood stories?

❀ Are you aware of any unhealthy messages you received during childhood that you're still holding onto? If so, what impact do they have on your daily life?

❀ How has the way you were parented directly impacted the way you parent your child?

Triggered Wounds

Parenting our own children will trigger our earlier developmental issues. At each stage of our children's development, our own unresolved developmental issues and unmet childhood needs will come up. Often, the result is toxic parenting.

—John Bradshaw, Homecoming

Children push our buttons. At times, on a daily basis. Our unbridled emotions take hold, and we react. It's these very buttons that trigger our emotions and result in our inability to parent rationally. As a result, we feel:

❀ Hopeless
❀ Helpless
❀ Inadequate
❀ Fearful
❀ Guilty[65]

When we react from an emotional place, we parent ineffectively. For example, when your child doesn't listen to you, you may feel disrespected, disregarded, or invisible. If you become emotionally charged when your child's behavior pushes your buttons, most likely you've experienced these feelings before. Perhaps you weren't heard or respected in your family. Maybe you had a boss who didn't listen to you. So your unhealed past is triggered by your child's apparent unwillingness to listen to you. Most likely your child hears you perfectly but chooses not to follow through on what you've asked them to do. This is a very normal behavior in children and can be frustrating for parents. However, you become angry or take it personally when your child doesn't listen simply because you've been reminded of painful unconscious feelings and memories—ones that you thought you'd put behind you many times before.

A mother attended one of my workshops, hoping to find the answer as to how to make her teenage son listen to her. She shared with the group that his behavior was driving her crazy. When I asked how his behavior made her feel, she quickly replied, "I'm angry." She also told us that she was resentful because after all she did for him, he didn't even have the common courtesy to listen to her or do what was asked of him.

After a while, I asked her again how this really made her feel. After a silent pause, she was able to drop beneath her initial answer of anger and state, "I feel unheard and totally disrespected." I asked the mother to stay with these feelings and to ask herself if she'd ever felt this way before, either as a child or during her adult years. She said no but then experienced an *aha* moment. She vividly remembered experiencing similar feelings in her relationship with her father and with her ex-husband. Suddenly, she began to laugh and said, "Oh my gosh, this is déjà vu!"

Until that moment, her repeated triggers and resulting anger had not been examined. Once she was able to identify the triggers and feelings that left her feeling vulnerable, she was able to alter her approach with her son. The willingness and courage to examine what lied beneath these triggers enabled her to wake up to how her past was affecting her ability to parent. She gained a better understanding of how her unresolved feelings kept her stuck in a pattern of knee-jerk reactions each time she was triggered.

Clearing your childhood wounds and dysfunctional patterns of behavior does not mean you push them out of the way, as if clearing a path. What it does mean is that you have the willingness and courage to look at unresolved feelings, limited thoughts, and beliefs that you might still be holding onto that are related to the way you were parented. Clearing and healing your wounds occurs in your willingness to uncover, unpack, and closely examine the wounds that have led to distorted perceptions and beliefs. This takes your willingness to work through them and to become intimate with your triggers—especially those that easily set you off on a daily or weekly basis. Rather than continuing to suppress your feelings, you learn to welcome them.

This can be scary and uncomfortable at first, but I urge you to do this for yourself and your child. Whether you choose to do this on your own or with the help of a professional, it will be time well spent. There are many resources available to help you. Some individuals are able to heal themselves without the help of others; however, this is not easy. Just as you wouldn't try to care for yourself medically, I believe your emotional health should be nurtured and healed with the help of professionals or a safe confidant.

Healing your past enables you to clear your path to freedom, both in your daily life and in your parenting. You will also relieve your child of carrying the same emotional burdens you've carried for most of your life—burdens that were never intended for them to carry.

Paul Levy, author, artist, and spiritual activist, states, "Parents cannot be expected to have no faults or unresolved complexes, which would be superhuman, but rather, they should make sincere efforts to not deny and repress their weak points and unconscious areas but recognize them for what they are." He says, "With regards to their unconscious issues, parents . . . 'should at least come to terms with them consciously; they should make it a duty to work out their inner difficulties for the sake of the children.'"[66]

Healing your wounds does not mean that the hurt and trauma you've experienced will vanish from your memory. You will still remember, but you'll learn to have a different relationship with it. The wound and associated feelings will no longer stop you in your tracks or inhibit your growth. Byron Katie, speaker and author, states, "The burden is never life; it's what you're thinking and believing about life."[67]

Your willingness to be vulnerable and to delve deeper into your places of "unfinished business" will help you heal and open you up to your authentic self. But first, it is imperative that you take time and begin the process to heal yourself within, to examine your *inner child*, the one who continues to unconsciously exist with wounds and unmet needs remaining from your childhood. The inner child tries to control your life in order to feel safe. It is time to let your inner child know that you are now an adult and are in charge. You are now able to take care of him or her and keep them safe.

John Bradshaw, author of *Homecoming: Reclaiming and Championing Your Inner Child*, refers to the process of healing as one of grief. This involves stages of grief, which include the following:

ⓥ Trust
- During this stage, you let your inner child know that they are safe and all feelings are accepted; you are there to support them.

ⓥ Validation
- Allow yourself to feel validated in your beliefs and feelings, to recognize that you were wounded by your parent simply because they too had been wounded as a child.

ⓥ Shock and anger
- Your ability to see your childhood and parents in reality may come as a shock to you, especially if you tried to sugarcoat it in the past. The pain and anger of seeing "what was" will allow you to move forward and consciously choose how you want to care for yourself and your child.

ⓥ Sadness
- Sadness is part of grieving—what could have been or what was. Allowing yourself to feel sadness will help you to heal and move forward.

⊛ Remorse
- Recognize and let go of your wish that you had done things differently. Realize that as a child, you were not capable of doing more.

⊛ Loneliness
- Due to shame that was inflicted on you as a child, you hid your true self—your essence. You hid your "self" from yourself and others. All in an effort to be loved. As a result, your true, hidden self developed a sense of loneliness. It is through meeting yourself, without fear and judgment, that healing begins.[68]

Parenting as a Whole

Life's stressors, such as marriage, the birth of a child, divorce, a job change, or death can easily trigger childhood issues. These events can generate stress under the best of circumstances, but our ability to handle stress as a parent is also dependent upon our parent's ability to parent us.

Your ability to navigate life as an adult and parent is influenced by how you were parented. Your foundation was set many years ago. How well you continue to "build" a life for yourself and your children depends on the strength of the foundation your parents provided for you. If you were raised in a dysfunctional family, your foundation is most likely shaky. You have an opportunity and a responsibility to rebuild this foundation now, one brick at a time. This rebuilding does not occur overnight but rather in small ways each day. You must let go of dysfunctional pieces of the foundation and replace it with a healthy structure—a structure that will sustain both you and your family for generations to come.

Parenting as a whole means parenting from your wholeness, first by being the parent for yourself that you did not have. It requires taking the time to understand and meet your own emotional needs now as an adult—needs that went unmet when you were a child. You're able to parent from wholeness when you rely on yourself to fulfill your needs rather than relying on your child, spouse, or parents to fulfill them for you. Once you're able to provide this for yourself, you're then able to wholeheartedly provide what your child needs.

But what do children really need to grow into healthy adults? According to Kimberlee Roth and Freda B. Friedman, PhD, LCSW, authors of *Surviving a Borderline Parent: How to Heal Your Childhood Wounds and Build Trust, Boundaries, and Self-Esteem*, there are "six seeds" needed to help grow healthy children:

- Support
- Respect and acceptance
- A voice
- Unconditional love and affection
- Consistency
- Security[69]

Although these may seem simple and obvious, parents are challenged on a daily basis to provide all of these. Even the most conscientious parent will not be able to meet all of their child's needs on a daily basis. Parents are not perfect—they are human. As a parent, you will lose your patience, regret an impulsive remark, or overreact. But hopefully, you'll be willing to apologize when you fall short.

When Carl Jung said, "The greatest burden a child must bear is the unlived life of the parents," he was not only referring to the negative impact of parents putting their life on hold for their child but also to the inner wounds that parents unconsciously carry with them, generational wounds that can infect and create harmful damage to their children.

The best gift you can offer your child is to do your own inner work, to heal within so that you can become whole once again. This is how you came into this world, and it is your birthright. The gift of wholeness is priceless, for you and your family. When you rediscover your innate joy and love for yourself, you release others from taking care of your emotional needs. Not only do you find freedom for yourself, but your child is also freed to become their own authentic self.

Journaling Exercises

- ✺ Have you been aware of your own inner child?

- ✺ Have you found it difficult to recognize and examine feelings you've suppressed? In what ways have you dealt with these unresolved feelings?

- ✺ After learning about the six seeds important for the growth of a healthy child, can you identify the seeds that you felt your parents provided for you?

- ✺ Identify two events in which your parents were able to provide one or more of the six seeds. Describe the event, your emotions surrounding the event, and what you learned from the event. Pay close attention to what your parents provided and how you benefited from their ability to do so.

- ✺ Now reflect on two occasions when any one of the six seeds was withheld or not given by your parents. Include the event, the surrounding circumstances, and your resulting feelings. What did you tell yourself about your experience? What was the resulting story you told when your needs were not met?

- ✺ How do you think this affected your development? Your ability to feel secure and loved?

- ✺ Were you able to be yourself when you were growing up? Or, looking back, were you not free to be you? Were you perhaps not quite sure who the real you was?

⊚   Were there other positive role models in your life? Others who
     provided support that helped foster your emotional growth? If
     so, who, and how did they support you?

⊚   Can you remember times when you've been able to offer these
     seeds to your own children? Identify two circumstances and
     the particular seeds that you offered. Describe your child's
     behavior and emotions. How did the seeds help nurture your
     child and foster their emotional growth?

⊚   Describe a time when you withheld any or all of the six seeds.
     (Please do so without self-judgment. We've all done this at
     times.) Describe your child's resulting emotions and behavior.
     Did they act out or withdraw? What do you think they took
     away from the event? What did you take away from the event?

⊚   If you had the opportunity to change your own behavior (and
     you always have the ability to do so), what would you change?
     How would you interact differently with your child?

⊚   Knowing what I know now, I intend to . . .

Chapter 11

Who's Taking Care of You?

There are days I drop words of comfort
on myself like falling leaves and remember
that it is enough to be taken care of by myself.

—Brian Andreas

*T*ypically, you don't recognize the symptoms of dehydration until you're suffering thirst. But research indicates that thirst is an indicator that you are already dehydrated. And while common sense tells you to drink water frequently throughout the day, even when you don't feel the need, as well as before and during activities, many of us don't drink water until we are thoroughly parched.

The same applies to self-care. Chances are you do not think about self-care until you're exhausted and running on fumes.

Chapter Summary

Many moms take care of others before caring for themselves. This deep-rooted behavior has been learned and instilled from generation to generation. So young women grow up and take their role as caregiver to heart. As a result, many mothers do not take care of their own needs because of their ingrained belief that self-care is selfish. Self-care is not selfish—it is selfless. Airline attendants tell mothers to put their own oxygen mask on first before helping their child, advice counterintuitive to most mothers. Self-care is not only important but also crucial to your well-being and that of your child, simply because you cannot give what *you* yourself do not have.

The Importance of Self-Care

Stephanie, a mother of two I'd been working with, looked at me with a blank stare when I asked her, "Who's taking care of you?" She appeared baffled by my question. Perhaps she was surprised because the focus of our conversation had been on her children rather than on her. I asked because she seemed completely overwhelmed and admitted to being so. As Stephanie described her litany of work and family responsibilities, I noticed she talked about the needs of her family, friends, and colleagues but not about her own.

I asked her again, "Who's taking care of you?" After a moment, Stephanie answered, "I guess no one is taking care of me, including *me*."

She began to cry as she told me that she didn't have a free moment in the day to think about herself. Stephanie began to realize that the more exhausted she became, the more she overreacted by yelling at her children. She looked defeated. Before having children, Stephanie had sworn she would never be like her own mother, who was a frequent yeller. Feelings of guilt weighed heavily on Stephanie's heart. And even if she did have time, Stephanie told me, putting her own needs first would be selfish and create more guilt.

Like many mothers, Stephanie had put her needs on the back burner. Maybe she intended to think about them in the future, but not quite yet. I've worked with many mothers who ignore their own needs in an effort to meet the needs of others. This focus on others before self becomes habitual and is so ingrained that mothers are often unaware of their own unmet needs. It's not until they experience burnout and have little left of themselves to give to others that they feel the effects of little to no self-care.

Self-care has become a buzzword, and there are many books written on the subject. The topic has been included in so many self-help books on the market that it has almost become cliché. However, there is good reason for it. Our lives have become so busy that we're not taking time to care for ourselves.

I ask mothers in my workshops, "Who takes care of mothers?" The participants often laugh and say, "No one!" However, the fact is that mothers can be their own best caregivers while still giving to others. In fact, mothers *are* the "who" in the question "Who is taking care of you?" And although they may be unaware of it, ultimately, mothers need to be the ones who take care of themselves, for they know best what restores them. I often remind them that, as Stephanie discovered, there is never time for self-care unless mothers themselves intentionally schedule it.

No one can recognize your need for self-care but you. So if you're waiting for someone to offer you free time each day for self-care, most likely it's not going to happen.

No one is going to help you create time for self-care until you recognize the importance of it and make it a priority—for you.

Please hear me out as I talk about the importance of self-care. It's critical not only for your well-being but also for that of your family. Self-care is an act of loving yourself. Self-care requires you to open your heart to yourself without judgment or guilt.

Perhaps this idea of self-care being a loving act is a new concept for you. Think of something that you have done for yourself in the past month. Not for anyone else, but for yourself. How did you feel after giving yourself this gift of self-care? Maybe you noticed you felt a bit lighter, not as weighed down by responsibilities. Some mothers I've worked with report feeling more openhearted and loving toward their children after doing something for themselves. It is a truism that what you appreciate appreciates.

Ali Miller, a therapist in Berkeley and San Francisco, California, says that self-care is "an attitude toward yourself that you matter, that your needs matter. . . . When we really believe in our own mattering, we want to take care of ourselves. . . . But if you don't believe this just yet, practicing self-care can help you develop a relationship with yourself that's more loving, kind, and caring."[70]

There are benefits to self-care:

- Self-care enables mothers to be better moms and caregivers
- Self-care sends a message to yourself that you matter and models for your family the importance of your needs
- Self-care reduces stress
- Self-care supports and improves physical and mental health
- Self-care helps you reconnect with yourself—and hear your inner voice
- Self-care helps you live more mindfully
- Self-care helps you recharge your batteries

When Self-Care Is Lacking

Meghan, a mother of three children, ages ranging from five to twelve, walked into my office with a low battery. She said during our first visit that her children's constant whining and fighting overwhelmed her. Meghan had a full-time career, which included travel. She reported that life was good, except for her children's behavior. Toward the end of our conversation, I asked her if she allowed any time during the day for herself. She laughed. "Who has time? I certainly don't!" Meghan quickly added that she felt fulfilled by her children and her career and didn't really feel the need to add anything else to her life, even if she did have the time. However, she also told me that she was exhausted at night and overwhelmed every morning just trying to get out the door. By the time she took her children to school and landed in her office (often late), her chest was tight as she faced her busy workday.

To help Meghan with her morning overwhelm, I suggested she create a ten-minute quiet time for herself each morning before she woke her children. Meghan was reluctant because, she said, the only way she could find the extra time was to get up ten minutes earlier. She exclaimed, "I'm already tired every morning when the alarm goes off, so I need that time to sleep!" Her interest piqued when I suggested the change could lead to an improvement in her children's behavior. So we spent time examining Meghan's busy schedule and daily responsibilities and found ways to shorten her evening to-do list so that she could get to bed earlier and get up ten minutes earlier.

Meghan eagerly committed to the new plan. She decided to delegate some of her evening chores to her children and husband. Although they resisted at first, they began to get on board and helped pick up the slack for Meghan. Her children began putting their school snacks and backpack together each evening and straightened the family room, and her husband offered to do the dinner dishes each evening. Meghan was unsure how long their willingness to help would last, but I challenged her to look at this as an experiment. Only after some time would she be able to determine the effectiveness of the ten-minute quiet time experiment. She agreed to try it for two weeks.

The following week, Meghan attended one of my parenting workshops. She was excited to share her good news: the experiment had worked, and after only one week, she felt much calmer and her children's behavior had improved dramatically! During the work-shop, she shared with the group how she had created a sense of calm in her household simply by asking her family to share the evening chores and giving herself the gift of ten minutes of quiet in the morning. She used the time to read, listen to music, or watch her backyard birds. Because she set the tone of calm at the beginning of her day, she became aware and intentional in creating other quiet moments throughout the day.

Because Meghan was overwhelmed, she focused on her children's behavior as the problem. She is not alone in this. It is human nature to blame others rather than to take responsibility for ourselves. It's much easier to believe that our children's behavior is causing the problem. Of course, children do whine and fight, but have you ever noticed that when you're on system overload, your children begin to act out? The exact time you need them to cooperate so your day will go smoothly is often precisely when they choose to disobey. You may even take your children's behavior personally, believing that they're acting out to punish you. The fact is that children are like sponges that soak up our energy, positive and negative. I often refer to them as little barometers in the family whose behavior indicates the ups and downs in your moods and energy. I explained that rather than causing her stress, Meghan's children were most likely responding to her own imbalanced feelings of being overwhelmed and exhausted.

When you are balanced, there is a much better chance your children will be too.

Your needs can coexist with the needs of your spouse and kids. Balance is created by intentional planning and taking everyone's needs into consideration. Naturally, there will be give and take—better yet, giving and receiving. On some days, more attention will be paid to a certain family member's needs rather than another's. For example, if your child is sick, you need to devote more time tending to his needs. And on some days, if one parent is absent, you will have to pick up the slack with extra responsibilities. But these times should be the exception, not the rule. In general, you should try to spread out the responsibility so that you can meet your family's needs while maintaining your own resources.

Tapping into your own emotions and energy level is the best way to notice your need for self-care. Providing self-care on a daily basis increases your odds of being able to manage your emotions during times of stress. And as a result, you'll experience less burnout! The next time you are tired or frustrated, remind yourself that it may be a perfect time to take a break, a time-out, or what I prefer to call a *time-off*.

Self-care is like taking a break for yourself. Self-care begins with you—not only on a physical level but also on an emotional level. Your emotional well-being is as important as your physical well-being. Research has shown that our physical health is directly affected by our emotional health. When I speak of emotional health, I am referring not only to your emotional state but also to your beliefs and the thoughts that influence your emotional health. It's difficult to uncover what those beliefs and thoughts are when you're on the go. The best way to tap into your subtle thinking and beliefs is to stop, get still, and dig deep. It's about allowing yourself to get in touch with your heart.

I've witnessed, professionally and personally, the detrimental effects when a mother's self-care is lacking. Fatigue and feelings of being overwhelmed are the common result. Mothers become prone to illness, physically and emotionally, when self-care has been neglected. It's often only then that mothers are forced to pay attention. Christiane Northrup, MD, a leading expert in women's health, states in the documentary *Hungry for Change*, "If we had a rampant epidemic of self-love, then our healthcare costs would go down dramatically."[71] Taking the time to love ourselves would decrease our susceptibility to many struggles.

When you are constantly giving to others, do you ever think about how much you're giving of yourself? How much of you are you giving away, and what part of yourself is actually left for you to share with your children? (Not in terms of doing more for them or giving them more stuff, but how you're showing up in the relationship.) Are you sharing your best part—your patient, kind, compassionate part? Or do you find that what your children see is what's left of you at the end of the day—your frustrated, negative, judgmental self? This is all you have left, simply because you haven't had or taken time to refill your own emotional tank (by relaxing and reconnecting with yourself). When you've been on system overload, constantly giving to others or struggling to keep up with daily life, how relaxed are you? I've worked with many children and teens, and most of them tell me that they just want their parents to be happy. They complain that their parents are stressed and seem upset most of the time. Is this how you want your children to experience you?

One of the other dangers in doing too much for others and not enough for yourself is resentment. When mothers express feeling "taken for granted or unappreciated," what they are often experiencing is a lack of appreciation for everything they do for their family. When feeling this way, mothers are apt to lash back at their children with, "How can you be this way, after *everything* I've done for you?" Kids are often confused by this question, because in their minds, they weren't asking for everything to be done for them.

I've also observed mothers who appear numb to life—to their children, their family, and themselves. At first glance, they appear fine. They describe their ability to forge ahead each day, doing what they need to do for their family. They simply go through the motions and do not feel any joy. Some mothers tell me they feel detached from life. Mothers experiencing the feelings of numbness to life or even detachment often wonder if they are depressed.

There is a link between lack of self-care and depression. Sometimes lack of self-care can mimic depressive symptoms or even lead to depression. I've worked with mothers who wonder if they're depressed. They describe experiencing occasional depressive symptoms. But what they mostly describe is feeling utterly lost and uncertain, unsure if they even want to be a mother anymore.

Although you may not have experienced these same feelings, chances are you've felt emotionally drained if your focus has been on doing for others at the expense of your own needs. In my work, this seems prevalent in women who have continually put others' needs before their own. This is not a new phenomenon, but today, mothers are more vocal about their frustration, exhaustion, and loss of self. Years ago, women were more apt to keep their feelings to themselves. Again, caring for your children without caring for yourself backfires. Striking a balance between good self-care (which includes setting boundaries for yourself) and caring for your kids creates a healthy balance for all.

The problem with putting your own needs last is that it often leaves you unable to recognize when you need self-care. And by the time you do realize your desperate need, your energy reserves are already depleted.

At that point, when your batteries have been allowed to run down, it is more difficult to recharge. Think of electronic devices. You don't wait until the battery is totally drained before you recharge it. You're no different. A rundown mom, like a rundown battery, is in-effective. When you're rundown, you are probably less patient with your children and apt to react harshly rather than respond in a loving way. When this happens, you may feel remorse or guilt about your short fuse.

The next time this happens, remind yourself that your batteries are running low and are signaling you to slow down or change direc-tion. It is a sign to not only change your emotional reactivity but also provide emotional support for yourself, through self-care.

These feelings affect the whole family. I ask all children what they would most want to change if they could change anything about their family. Many express frustration about their mother's stress level, and most say they wish their moms would relax and have more fun. These kids are focusing on what's really important in life.

When time is limited and you're faced with the choice of spending time with your children or finishing everything on your to-do list, what do you choose? Most mothers try to squeeze too many respon-sibilities into too little time, and they ramp up their efforts as soon as the kids are in bed. Your kids don't care if the house is in perfect order or that the laundry is done—they care about having a mom who is relaxed and enjoys spending time with them. The next time your child asks you to play with them, please do. Play has the power to create joy, deepen connection, and enhance relationships. You'll be sending a message to your child that they matter, and when you play with your kids, you're practicing self-care. Play raises your endorphins (the feel-good drug) and helps calm you down.

Why Self-Care Is Difficult

Women and mothers have created, consciously and unconsciously, many reasons and excuses to justify their behavior in ignoring their own needs. Many mothers are resistant to my advice to include self-care in their daily lives. Some women view themselves primarily as mothers; it's become their sole identity, and it's difficult for them to look beyond the needs of their children. Although their initial response varies, the theme is often the same: "I don't have the time or energy to think about myself. It's all I can do to meet the needs of my children, let alone mine!" They may hope for a few minutes for themselves at the end of the day. They fall into bed at night too tired to consider anything other than sleep only to wake up the next morning and hop on the treadmill of life. Many mothers are living their daily lives on this continuous treadmill, only stopping, or falling off, when exhaustion sets in. These mothers feel exhausted and overwhelmed but are at a loss as to how to improve their lives.

Self-care is often difficult for mothers because they view it as selfish to put their own needs before their children's. I remind them that when they take a shower (a short one, of course, before they're back to taking care of their kids), they are honoring their body with self-care. When they sleep at night, they are engaged in self-care. Mothers hesitantly agree with this concept but insist that anything more than meeting their own basic needs would be indulgent.

Sadly, self-care has gotten confused with "selfishness." Self-centeredness and selfishness preclude taking care of others, which of course is part of mothers' lives. *Self-care*, on the other hand—taking care of yourself physically, mentally, and emotionally—does not preclude caring for others.

Self-care is never a selfish act—it is simply good stewardship of the only gift I have, the gift I was put on earth to offer to others. Anytime we can listen to true self and give the care it requires, we do it not only for ourselves but for the many others whose lives we touch.

—*Parker Palmer,* Let Your Life Speak: Listening for the Voice of Vocation

Even mothers who recognize the importance of self-care rarely seem to find the time to practice it for themselves. They may have good intentions to include self-care in their daily life, but usually they continue to put their own needs last. What mothers often tell me is that if they only have a five- or ten-minute window of free time, and that's just not enough, why bother? And yet even a few minutes each day devoted to self-care are better than none.

Think of a time when you took just a minute to look at beautiful clouds, or watch an ocean wave, or laugh at a puppy chasing its tail. Did you notice a shift in your energy afterward? Chances are, just stopping for that minute to engage in something that didn't require activity or thought brought you a little peace or joy.

Most mothers' calendars are overfilled. Mothers are busy being busy. We all suffer from busyness. Busyness has an addictive nature. Some very busy mothers tell me they can't imagine living any other way. They almost get a rush from their frenzied schedules, running from one activity to another. I once worked with a mother and daughter who were overscheduled and on system overload. They had at least five activities each day, most of them for her daughter. They had no downtime to relax and just be, and the mother had no time for self-care. She was very anxious and told me that her daughter was exhibiting anxious behaviors too. When I suggested to the mom that she and her daughter were on activity overload, she said it was important to her and her daughter and she was not willing to make any changes. However, should this mother choose to make self-care a priority, they could both find spare, quiet moments, even sitting at a red light on the way to her daughter's ballet lesson, that might relieve their sense of overload.

Whether you are a stay-at-home mom or have a full-time career, life will always be busy. The busyness will take over if you allow it. It's not until you closely examine your day, pare down your schedule, and have the courage to slow down that will you find the necessary time to meet your own needs.

What I often hear from mothers who are crazy busy is that they are drowning in their busyness. Their responsibilities have multiplied exponentially, and they are tired and overwhelmed. However, some mothers tell me that they're afraid to stop and just be. They are afraid of what might come to the surface of their minds if they are still. They are afraid to examine their own thoughts and feelings—afraid they won't like what they see, as if trying to outrun their thoughts will keep them at bay. There is a price to pay when you run from yourself. Your *fear* of discovering what lies within yourself often outweighs the actual *freedom* you'll discover: freedom from what might be dragging you down; freedom to make conscious choices to improve your life. Taking time for self-care and self-reflection will not hurt or make things worse, and running from them certainly won't help.

What Self-Care Looks Like—for Yourself

Self-care is not about adding something to your to-do list. It's about cultivating a kinder, gentler relationship with yourself.

—*Renée Trudeau, author and coach*

Self-care is a form of self-love. Besides avoiding emotions, most people also tend to stay in their heads, allowing their thoughts to circle around and around, often stuck in a mental haze. However, when you allow yourself to be comfortable in the silence, that's when feelings begin to arise. From that quiet space, you're more likely to sense how you're feeling and gain a better understanding of what you need. This takes time and practice. When you're truly in touch with your feelings and beliefs, you can make choices that are beneficial to you—intentional choices that help you live your life with more ease—because you will be aligned in heart, body, and mind. When you're in alignment, internally and externally, not only will you be at peace, but most likely, those around you will too as they pick up on your calm, positive energy. This quiet alignment is necessary for self-care. No one can possibly know what you need better than you. However, it's not until you take time to self-reflect that you're able to determine what type of self-care fits you best.

There may be circumstances that do not make some types of self-care possible. For example, single mothers and mothers with financial constraints or unsupportive husbands may not have the luxury of a babysitter to ensure outings for themselves. Mothers with multiple children or children with special needs may find it difficult to even find time for themselves. However, in my many years working with mothers, I can attest that mothers who wanted to begin to care for themselves found a way to make it happen. Initially, time devoted to themselves may have been only two minutes, but in that short time, they created a self-care ritual. Self-care became a priority for these mothers. They reported that they fiercely protected this time because they knew how important it was to their mental and physical well-being. When money was not available for self-care, mothers found simple ways (that cost only pennies) to treat themselves. A bubble bath, after the kids were in bed, was a luxurious treat that set the tone for a relaxing evening.

Mothers who protected their self-care time also recognized positive effects on their children's emotions and behavior as a result of their initiation of self-care. The ripple effect of self-care is huge. Your gift of self-care will have a positive effect on your family.

So let's talk about your family's needs and how they can coexist with your own. Let's assume you won't find empty time slots in your day to meet everyone's needs, so you'll need to look at ways to create the time. You'll also need to identify your own needs. No one can read your mind; only you will be able to determine those needs. Write down your most basic needs and then any others you'd like to include— although you may not be able to include them on a daily basis, it's nice to have a wish list of needs to choose from.

I invite you to begin caring for yourself, and I challenge you to do it for yourself. If you find yourself resistant to the idea, I'll remind you that the consequence of not taking care of yourself is your diminished ability to take care of anyone else. It must start with you. And you'll gain a deeper connection with yourself as well as your family.

The most powerful relationship you will ever have is the relationship with yourself.

—*Steve Maraboli*, Life, the Truth, and Being Free

Beyond scheduled and random acts of self-care, I also urge you to stop and drop your busyness. Stop what you're doing right now (yes, even while you're reading this book) and slowly take three deep breaths (inhale through your nose and out through your mouth, very deep breaths that go all the way down to your belly). When you do this, you may immediately notice a shift. When you give your mind a rest, you offer yourself a gift of "calm" and you feel better.

Journaling Exercises

When you focus your time and effort on meeting only the needs of others, you're left with very little time to focus on yourself. Remember, you cannot give what you do not have! Write your thoughts about the following questions below.

- When was the last time you allowed yourself to think about your own needs and desires without feeling guilty?

- If you had an extra ten to fifteen minutes for yourself during the day, how would you spend the time? List five different ways to nurture yourself.

- What are your thoughts about self-care as an act of self-love?

- Do you know any women who practice self-care? List them and describe how they take care of themselves. Can you see ways that they benefit from practicing self-care? (Afterward, consider giving one or two of these women a call and asking about how they manage to take care of themselves and the benefits of doing so.)

- Do you ever ask others for help? If not, what's stopping you? If so, what response have you received?

- How do you typically spend your day? Make two columns below. Title the first *What I have to do* and the second *What I'd like to do*. After you have studied your lists, drop one item from your *have to do* list (one that won't cause harm if dropped). Now look at the blank space you created in the column. How does it feel to see an empty space, some extra time in your day? Try filling it with one item from your *like to do* list.

- How easy or hard was it to drop a *have to do* activity? How did you feel when you added a *like to do* activity?

⊛   Over the next week, set your intention to make time for a few things on your *like to do* list. Feel free to change the activity when you're inspired to do so. Mix it up and have fun! Journal below about how your day changed after experiencing some *like to do* moments.

⊛   What do you need in order to give yourself permission to follow through on your *like to do* activity?

⊛   Now look at your *have to do* list and choose three activities that you can delegate to your family (remember that giving children responsibilities empowers them and teaches them to be responsible individuals). Now that you've lightened your *have to do* list, what can you add to your *like to do* list?

⊛   What do you need in order to create an extra ten to fifteen minutes each day for yourself?

⊛   List three ways you think you will benefit from practicing self-care.

⊛   How do you think your family will benefit if you take care of yourself? Be as specific as possible.

⊛   Take a quiet moment to pause. Take three deep breaths all the way down to your belly. Write your answers to the following questions.

⊛   How am I feeling right now?

⊛   What are my needs in this moment?

⊛   Can I honor one of my needs?

⊛   Knowing what I know now, I intend to . . .

Chapter 12

You Have All the Answers . . . When You Really Listen

Your heart knows things that your mind can't explain.

—Unknown

*G*ripping the outer bathroom doorknob, I *knew* my dad was on the other side of the door and something was very wrong. I kept pounding on the door, yet something told me—a voice I heard in my mind said—*Do not open that door.* I ran to get my mom and said, "He's gone." My choice of words still haunts me. Only an hour earlier, my dad had come home from work and was going to help me start the lawn mower after he changed his clothes. When he didn't return, I went upstairs to remind him. I couldn't find him but saw the closed bathroom door. When my mom finally opened the door, she discovered that my forty-four-year-old dad had died of a massive heart attack. Although I experienced a momentary pang of guilt because I hadn't opened the door, I *knew* in that moment I was never supposed to open it. The doctor later assured me it was already too late. After his death, I *knew* I was never supposed to see my dad like this—it was not to be my last memory.

I *knew* my sixteen-year-old daughter was lying to me when she said she was going to a friend's house to spend the night. I wanted to trust her, so I let her go. My inner voice said *Call her friend's parent*, yet I didn't want my daughter to feel I didn't trust her. But I *knew*. The truth, my *inner* truth, was revealed the following day when I received a call that there had been a party, with underage drinking, and that my daughter was involved.

I also *knew* when my second daughter was pregnant the day before she told me. I longed to be a grandmother, and I tried to talk myself out of my *inner knowing*. I rationalized that because I wanted to hear this news, my mind was tricking me, only to find out the next day that indeed she was pregnant and my dream of being a gramma was coming true! Intuition is usually spot on, but you may not recognize it until after the fact.

Years ago, my work as a pediatric nurse practitioner confirmed my belief in intuition—specifically, a mother's intuition. I knew my own mom intuition had not failed me, so I was certainly going to honor the intuition of a mother whose children I cared for. One morning, I was working in the clinic and met with a mom and her fifteen-year-old daughter, who was scheduled for a sports physical. The mother asked if I'd take a look at a mole on her daughter's back. I did, and although I wasn't concerned because it looked fairly regular in size and shape with no change in pigmentation, I referred her to a dermatologist to evaluate the mole. I did this for one reason only: because I heard the mom say, "I just have this feeling that something is not right."

I could have relied on my own clinical judgment, which would've led me to believe that the mole was not cancerous. However, my own inner voice told me to listen to this mom's intuition. It was worth the risk of being told by the dermatologist that the consult was unnecessary. My patient, a fifteen-year-old girl, was diagnosed with melanoma—certainly not a typical diagnosis for a girl this young. Luckily, it was discovered early and she survived a potentially deadly diagnosis. I'm grateful to share this happy ending—all because of a mother's *intuition*. Many of the pediatricians I worked with were male. Although they listened to mothers, most of them did not take a mother's intuition into account. They were scientifically trained, and intuition was not part of their medical school curriculum. I remember telling a few of my colleagues: if a mom has a gut feeling about her child, *listen*.

What is intuition? According to the *Oxford Dictionary*, intuition is "the ability to understand something immediately, without the need for conscious reasoning."[72] Intuition is often referred to as the "sixth sense." The other five senses we use to perceive or sense are hearing, sight, taste, smell, and touch. These are commonly recognized, and we depend on them on a daily basis. What is often not talked about is the "sixth sense."

Mark Nepo, poet, philosopher, and author of *Seven Thousand Ways to Listen*, states, "The way we think and feel and sense our way into all we don't know is the art of intuition. It is an art of discovery." He adds, "*To intuit means to look upon, to instruct from within, to understand or learn by instinct*."[73] All humans have an intuitive ability, but it is not often developed. Because it's not as recognized as the other five senses, it's often not talked about—and some don't believe in intuition. Yet we are all intuitive beings and can gain a lot of insight when we pay attention. Yes, I believe *mothers do know best.* So why do they themselves or others discount their inner knowing?

> The intuitive mind is a sacred gift, and the rational mind is a faithful servant. We have created a society that honors the servant and has forgotten the gift.
>
> —*Unknown*

Because intuition is not tangible or visible, we often discount its validity. As a society, we are more in our head and less in our heart. Because some view intuition as "woo woo" or "out there," it's not often discussed. And even if you've acknowledged having this "knowing," you might have brushed it off as a coincidence. How many times have you ignored your own inner signal? You may have had a gut feeling or a tug in your heart. It's easy to let life's interruptions distract you from your inner knowing. Most likely, you've not honed your intuitive skills. Between your busy everyday life and the lack of recognition in intuition, it's easy to forget about it.

Psychiatrist Dr. Judith Orloff, author of *Guide to Intuitive Healing,* says, "Mother's intuition is the deep intuitive blood bond a mother can have with her child," and "it is a sixth sense mothers have that the child may be in danger or in need."[74] Mothers have recognized their intuitive connection with their kids for many centuries. Recently, there's been research reporting that mothers actually have DNA of their offspring in their bloodstream and brain, DNA that resides in a mother's brain for decades. A ninety-four-year-old mother was found to have her son's DNA in her brain. I've wondered whether this phenomenon actually increases the intuitive connection between a mother and her child. Does it in fact strengthen the heartstrings between them? Could this boost a mom's *intuitive* ability?

Can you remember a time when you were worried about your child and took them took them to the doctor only to be told they were fine—when you knew they weren't? Perhaps you left the office with a nagging feeling that something wasn't right. When you decided the next day to revisit the doctor for a second look, you weren't surprised when the doctor confirmed your suspicion. Dr. Michael Howard, a pediatrician with over thirty years' experience, credited a mother for saving her son's life. Feeling that something was not right with her son, the mom didn't dismiss her nagging feeling even after being told by Dr. Howard that his exam and lab tests were normal. Fortunately, this mom persisted and brought her son back into the office a month later. Further lab tests were performed, and the six-year-old little boy was diagnosed with leukemia.[75] A research study cited in *The Lancet*, a well-respected medical journal, suggested that physicians should pay close attention to a mother's intuition. Dr. Orloff concurs with the study, claiming she too has seen the validity of a mother's intuition in her clinical work.[76]

Dr. Victor Shamas, a psychologist at the University of Arizona, also recognizes the importance of a mother's intuition. He regards intuition as "knowing something without knowing *how* you know." Dr. Shamas states, "I cannot say that universally being a mother increases your intuitiveness, but it's hard to deny the intuitive connection a mother has with their child."[77]

> The human heart feels things the eyes cannot see, and knows what the mind cannot understand.
>
> —*Robert Valett*

Whether you refer to your knowing as intuition, a heart or gut feeling, or unconscious knowledge, you have the ability, and you need to pay attention to that little voice in your head.

Follow your instincts on what you think your family needs and not what others expect. Your instincts are the best tool you have as a parent.

—*The Jenny Evolution*

It's important to educate yourself as a mom, to utilize the resources available to you to determine various options for you and your children. After you ascertain information and resources, tap into your own intuitive wisdom. See what feels right for you. Many mothers continue to look outside themselves for answers. Perhaps they believe others know more than they do. Or they look for validation. Keep in mind: your own intuition is a powerful resource—and it's readily available to you. Glinda, the good witch in *The Wizard of Oz*, reminded Dorothy, "You had the power all along." And so do you. When you learn to trust yourself, you no longer need validation from others. The opinions of others will matter less to you than your own. You may still seek outside guidance, but ultimately you'll choose what is right for you and your child. Mothers who learn to rely on their intuition often feel more relaxed. Because they trust their intuition, they feel empowered and confident. Although a mother's intuition does not provide her a crystal ball or a guaranteed outcome, it does enable her to say *I made the best decision based on what I felt was right at the time.*[78]

Journaling Exercises

- What are your thoughts and beliefs about intuition?

- Have you ever had a nagging feeling or thought that you chose to ignore? If so, what was the outcome?

- Has your intuitive ability changed since you became a mom? If so, how?

⊗ How has your intuition served you as a mom?

⊗ Identify a time when you followed your gut, your inner knowing. What was the result?

⊗ Reflect on a time when you ignored your intuition. Did you regret it? Why?

Listen to Your Heart

> There is a voice that doesn't use words.
> Listen.
>
> —*Rumi*

You have an intuitive ability, yet you may not have tapped into it. Developing intuition is a bit like going to the gym. Just as you work out to develop and strengthen your muscles, strengthening your intuition takes time and practice. It also takes a willingness to be open to the possibility of intuition: when you have a thought that something's just not right; when you're trying to make a decision yet have an uneasy feeling; when you have a sudden thought to call a girlfriend and a moment later, your friend calls you. These are all intuitive messages— your inner voice trying to get your attention.

The best way to pay attention is to be still. Take some time each day to be quiet. If you can only afford five minutes with your busy schedule, begin there. Take a break from electronics (unplug your phone, shut down your computer) and be still. You don't have to meditate or sit in complete silence if that doesn't resonate with you; you can take a walk, look up at the sky, or take a bath. My intuitive moments often occur in the shower when all I hear is the water falling from the shower head. I've realized of late that when I listen to music while showering, I miss out on the intuitive messages I often receive. However you're able to slow down your mind and open your heart, gift yourself those daily moments. When you're able to let go of life's distractions, sensory overload, and the chatter in your brain, your inner wisdom awaits. Initially, your "monkey mind" may chatter incessantly as your thoughts continue to swirl through your brain, but just keep breathing slowly. Envision the thoughts as clouds in the sky, slowly drifting by you. With each slow, relaxing breath, you're giving your mind permission to slow down too.

> Intuition literally means learning from within. Most of us were not taught how to use this sense, but all of us know well that 'gut' feeling. Learn to trust your inner feeling and it will become stronger. Avoid going against your better judgment or getting talked into things that just don't feel right.
>
> —*Doe Zantamata*

Your body sends you signals all day long. Pay attention to them. That tight feeling in your throat, chest, or abdomen may be giving you a signal. When your breath shortens or your heart races, this might be your signal to slow down. Maybe you're overwhelmed. Or your body might be trying to tell you that you need to slow down before making a decision, that the decision you're about to make may not be in your best interest.

When I've been on system overload, filling my plate too full and trying to accomplish the next task, my body speaks to me—usually with an illness or injury. You, too, might remember when you've received those inner messages or reminders to slow down. Yet perhaps you felt the need to push yourself—to forge ahead, even at the risk of your own well-being. Maybe you felt you'd be letting others down if you didn't follow through on a promise you made (even if you promised to take on more than was humanly possible). Often, it's in hindsight that you realize you've been sent messages all along—first as a whisper, and when you didn't listen, the inner voice became relentless, but you still didn't listen, most likely because you doubted your own intuition. When you learn to listen to the quiet messages, you won't have to deal later on with the screaming ones. Either way, your intuition will try to get your attention![79]

Your intuitive guidance will not be fear-based. If you find yourself acting out of fear, most likely your brain has kicked into gear, creating your fearful thoughts. Your inner critic, that inner voice, may be saying, *You can't do that! What are you, crazy?* Your ego, your inner critic, wants you to be logical and rational and to take the safe route, even when your heart is telling you differently. I recently saw this Facebook post:

> "Maybe we are here to love wildly, passionately, and fearless-ly," whispered the heart.
> "You are going to get us all killed!" yelled the brain.[80]

Your brain often lives in fear. Learn to trust your intuitive heart.

Your intuition speaks to you every day, but it often gets lost in the midst of life's noise. The only way to find time for quiet, intuitive listening is to create it. Your intuitive voice can be your tour guide throughout life, but only if you're available to listen. Otherwise, you may be making choices blindly moment to moment, day to day. None of us are guaranteed outcomes in life, but we do play a major part in our own life. You have the ability to gather information and make informed decisions—and your intuition is there to help guide you.

Here are some tips and reminders to help you cultivate your intuitive listening:

- Trust yourself—you have the answers
- Slow down, relax, and breathe
- Pay attention to thoughts and ideas that come to you—and any signal your body may send

- ֍ Move your body to help shift the energy from your brain into your physical body
- ֍ Ask for guidance, be patient, and listen[81]

Journaling Exercises

- ֍ Knowing what I know now, I intend to . . .

No one knows your children as well as you do. It takes courage to trust your intuition, but the more you listen to your intuition, the more you'll learn to trust it. When you learn to trust your intuition, you learn to trust yourself. You'll find you will begin to trust your own *knowing* as a mom and rely more on yourself and less on others. You'll begin to relax more, to feel more centered, calm, and confident. That is when you can really begin to tap into the joy of motherhood.

Wishing you courage, peace, and joy as you continue your journey of motherhood!

Bonnie

Notes

1. McConnell, Allen R. "The Social Self: Reflection Critical for Self-Improvement." PsychologyToday.com, September 18, 2010. https://www.psychologytoday.com/blog/the-social-self/201009/reflection-critical-self-improvement.

2. Senior, Jennifer. *All Joy and No Fun: The Paradox of Modern Parenthood*. New York: HarperCollins, 2015.

3. Wilson, Katherine. "Hopes and Dreams for My Child." *MummyPinkWellies.com* (site discontinued).

4. Geary, Kevin. "5 Ways to Help Your Children Turn Their Dreams into Reality." PickitheBrain.com, February 18, 2008. https://www.pickthebrain.com/blog/5-ways-to-help-your-children-turn-their-dreams-into-reality/.

5. Zakrzewski, Vicki. "How to Help Students Develop Hope." *Greater Good: The Science of a Meaningful Life*, November 6, 2012. http://greatergood.berkeley.edu/article/item/how_to_help_students_develop_hope.

6. Definition of preconceive. *Merriam-Webster*. http://www.merriam-webster.com/dictionary/preconceive.

7. Brown, Brené. Rising Strong: The Reckoning. The Rumble. The Revolution. New York: Spiegel & Grau, 2015.

8. Melton, Glennon Doyle. *Carry On, Warrior: The Power of Embracing Your Messy, Beautiful Life*. New York: Scribner, 2013.

9. Schulz, Kathryn. "On Being Wrong." TED talk, April 2011. https://www.ted.com/talks/kathryn_schulz_on_being_wrong/transcript?language=en.

10. Berry, William. "The Truth Will Not Set You Free." PsychologyToday.com,

May 6, 2012. https://www.psychologytoday.com/blog/the-second-noble-truth/201205/the-truth-will-not-set-you-free.

11. Achor, Shawn. "The Happy Secret to Better Work." TED talk, February 2012. http://www.ted.com/talks/shawn_achor_the_happy_secret_to_better_work/transcript?language=en.

12. Studna, Carl. *Click!: Choosing Love One Frame at a Time*. Los Angeles: Agape Media International, LLC., 2012.

13. Thompson, Kathryn. *Drops of Awesome: The You're-More-Awesome-Than-You-Think Journal*. Sanger, CA: Familius, 2014.

14. "*The Oprah Show*'s Greatest Lessons." Oprah.com, May 13, 2011. http://www.oprah.com/oprahshow/The-Greatest-Lessons-on-The-Oprah-Show_1.

15. Katie, Byron. *Loving What Is: Four Questions That Can Change Your Life*. New York: Three Rivers Press, 2003.

16. Schwarz, Nicole. "11 Mixed Messages Parents Send (and How to Stop)." ImperfectFamilies.com, January 21, 2014. https://imperfectfamilies.com/11-mixed-messages-parents-send-and-how-to-stop/.

17. Ibid.

18. Brown, Brené. *Daring Greatly: How the Courage to Be Vulnerable Transforms the Way We Live, Love, Parent, and Lead*. New York: Avery, 2012.

19. Brown, Brené. *The Gifts of Imperfection: Let Go of Who You Think You're Supposed to Be and Embrace Who You Are*. Center City, MN.: Hazelden, 2012.

20. Tsabary, Shefali. "Why Shaming Your Children Is a Bad Idea and What You Can Do Instead." *Huffington Post*, June 17, 2015. http://www.huffingtonpost.com/shefali-tsabary/why-shaming-your-children-is-a-bad-idea-and-what-you-can-do-instead_b_7579476.html.

21. Silin, Peter S. "Shame: The Emotion That Runs Us and Ruins Relationships." Counsellor-Coach.Ca. http://www.counsellor-coach.ca/articles-shame.htm.

22. Definition of guilt. *Merriam-Webster*. http://www.merriam-webster.com/dictionary/guilt.

23. Taffel, Ron. "Parenting Style: The Negative Messages That Even Good Parents Send." Parents.com, 2004 (from *Parents Magazine*, October 2000). http://www.parents.com/parenting/better-parenting/style/negative-messages-that-even-good-parents-send/.

24. McBride, Karyl. "Shaming Children Is Emotionally Abusive." PsychologyToday.com, September 10, 2012. https://www.psychologytoday.com/blog/the-legacy-distorted-love/201209/shaming-children-is-emotionally-abusive.

25. Brown, *The Gifts of Imperfection*.

26. Middelton-Moz, Jane. *Shame and Guilt: Masters of Disguise*. Deerfield Beach, FL.: Health Communications, Inc., 1990.

27. Brown, Brené. *I Thought It Was Just Me: Women Reclaiming Power and Courage in a Culture of Shame*. New York: Gotham Books, 2007.

28. Stafford, Rachel Macy.

29. Greenwood, Beth. "The Baumrind Theory of Parenting Styles." OurEveryday-Life.com. www.oureverydaylife.com/baumrind-theory-parenting-styles-6147.html.

30. Leo, Pam. *Connection Parenting: Parenting Through Connection Rather than Coercion, Through Love Instead of Fear*, 2nd ed. Deadwood, OR: Wyatt-MacKenzie Publishing, 2007.

31. Morman, Emily. "25 Years of Parenting: A Look Back and Ahead." MetroParent.com, January 8, 2015. http://www.metroparent.com/daily/parenting/parenting-issues-tips/25-years-parenting-look-back-ahead/.

32. Ibid.

33. Tsabary, Shefali. *The Conscious Parent: Transforming Ourselves, Empowering Our Children*. Vancouver, Canada: Namaste Publishing, 2010.

34. Leo, *Connection Parenting*.

35. Ethan Hawke BBC interview with Jane O'Brien. "Ethan Hawke Talks Sex, Death, and Knights." BBC.com, November 13, 2015. http://www.bbc.com/news/world-us-canada-34805223.

36. Fraser-Thrill, Rebecca. "What Is the Definition of Individuation?" VeryWell.com, updated April 19, 2016. https://www.verywell.com/individuation-3288007.

37. Jon Kabat-Zinn. *Wherever You Go, There You Are: Mindfulness Meditation in Everyday Life*. New York: Hyperion, 1994.

38. Runkel, Hal. *ScreamFree Parenting: The Revolutionary Approach to Raising Your Kids by Keeping Your Cool*. New York: Harmony Books, 2008.

39. Ibid.

40. Ibid.

41. Lancer, Darlene. "7 Parenting Essentials." WhatIsCodependency.com, 2012. https://www.whatiscodependency.com/7-parenting-essentials/.

42. Siegel, Daniel J., and Tina Payne Bryson. *No-Drama Discipline: The Whole-Brain Way to Calm the Chaos and Nurture Your Child's Developing Mind*. . New York: Bantam, 2014.

43. Tsabary, Shefali. *Out of Control: Why Disciplining Your Child Doesn't Work—and What Will.* Vancouver, Canada: Namaste Publishing, 2013.

44. Siegel and Bryson, *No-Drama Discipline.*

45. Tsabary, *Out of Control.*

46, Runkel, *ScreamFree Parenting.*

47. Bronson, Po. "Learning to Lie." *New York Magazine*, February 10, 2008. http://nymag.com/news/features/43893.

48. Ibid, p. 2.

49. Stiffelman, Susan. "Kids and Lying: How Can I Get My Son to Tell the Truth?" *HuffingtonPost.com*, November 4, 2011. http://www.huffingtonpost.com/2011/11/04/kids-and-lying-how-can-i-_n_1075016.html.

50. Roberts, Kate. "When Parents Lie." PsychologyToday.com, June 15, 2014. https://www.psychologytoday.com/blog/savvy-parenting/201406/when-parents-lie.

51. Handler, Suzanne. "5 Reasons Why Keeping Family Secrets Could Be Harmful." PyschCentral.com, August 22, 2013. http://psychcentral.com/blog/archives/2013/08/22/5-reasons-why-keeping-family-secrets-could-be-harmful/.

52. Imber-Black, Evan. *The Secret Life of Families.* New York: Bantam, 1998.

53. Brown, *Daring Greatly.*

54. Williams, Margery. *The Velveteen Rabbit.* London: Heinemann, 1922.

55. Wells, Jonathan. "Do You Have the Courage to Be Honest?" AdvancedLifeSkills.com. http://advancedlifeskills.com/blog/courage-to-be-honest/.

56. Brock, Farnoosh. "Develop Self-Confidence: 7 Lies You Need to Stop Telling Yourself." TinyBuddha.com. http://tinybuddha.com/blog/self-confidence-7-lies-you-need-to-stop-telling-yourself/.

57. "Momastery Blogger Glennon Doyle Melton on the One Habit All Successful Women Share." *The Huffington Post*, October 16, 2014. http://www.huffingtonpost.com/2014/10/16/momastery-glennon-doyle-melton-successful-women_n_5992298.html.

58. Kondo, Marie. *The Life-Changing Magic of Tidying Up: The Japanese Art of Decluttering and Organizing.* Berkeley, CA: Ten Speed Press, 2014.

59. Brown, *Daring Greatly.*

60. Brhel, Rita. "Prepare for Parenting by Healing Your Childhood Wounds." PsychCentral.com. http://blogs.psychcentral.com/attachment/2014/01/prepare-for-parenting-by-healing-your-childhood-wounds/.

61. Truman, Karol K. *Feelings Buried Alive Never Die*. St. George, UT: Olympus Distributing, 2002.

62. Hendrix, Harville, and Helen LaKelly Hunt. *Getting the Love You Want*. Soulful-Living.com. http://www.soulfulliving.com/love_you_want.htm.

63. McBride, Karyl. "Will I Ever Be Good Enough?" PsychologyToday.com, February 17, 2013. https://www.psychologytoday.com/blog/the-legacy-distorted-love/201302/will-i-ever-be-good-enough.

64. Miller, Alice. *The Drama of the Gifted Child: The Search for the True Self*, revised ed. New York: Basic Books, 2007.

65. Pincus, Debbie. "How to Stop Yelling at Your Kids: Use These 10 Tips." EmpoweringParents.com. https://www.empoweringparents.com/article/how-to-stop-yelling-at-your-kids-use-these-10-tips/.

66. Levy, Paul. "Unlived Lives." AwakenintheDream.com, 2010. http://www.awakeninthedream.com/unlived-lives/.

67. Katie, Byron. "The Burden Is . . ." ByronKatie.com, February 26, 2016. http://www.byronkatie.com/2016/02/the-burden-is/.

68. Borchard, Therese J. "6 Steps to Help Your Inner Child." PsychCentral.com. http://psychcentral.com/blog/archives/2012/09/23/6-steps-to-help-heal-your-inner-child/.

69. Roth, Kimberlee, and Freda B. Friedman. *Surviving a Borderline Parent: How to Heal Your Childhood Wounds and Build Trust, Boundaries, and Self-Esteem*. Oakland, CA: New Harbinger Publications, 2003.

70. Tartakovsky, Margarita. "What Self-Care Looks Like." PsychCentral.com. http://psychcentral.com/blog/archives/2015/03/15/what-self-care-looks-like/.

71. Northrup, Christiane. "The Power of Love." HungryforChange.tv. http://www.hungryforchange.tv/artice/the-power-of-love.

72. Definition of intuition. *Oxford Living Dictionaries*. https://en.oxforddictionaries.com/definition/intuition.

73. Nepo, Mark. *Seven Thousand Ways to Listen: Staying Close to What Is Sacred*. New York: Free Press, 2012.

74. Orloff, Judith. *Dr. Judith Orloff's Guide to Intuitive Healing: 5 Steps to Physical, Emotional, and Sexual Wellness*. New York: Three Rivers Press, 2000.

75. Brockway, Laurie Sue. "6 Things to Know about Mother's Intuition." PGEveryday.com, May 4, 2015. https://www.pgeveryday.com/family-life/parenting/article/6-things-to-know-about-mothers-intuition.

76. "Following Your Mother's Intuition." MommyFleur.com, March 23, 2013.

http://mommyfleur.com/2013/03/23/closed-following-your-mothers-intuition-expomom-2013-with-a-giveaway/.

77. Brasfield, Morgan. "Mother's intuition: Why we should follow our 'gut feelings.'" Today.com, April 18, 2013. http://www.today.com/parents/mothers-intuition-why-we-should-follow-our-gut-feelings-1C9504706.

78. Witter, Lisa. "4 Reasons Why Mother's Intuition Is Important in Everyday Parenting." IntuitiveParenting.com, June 6, 2015. http://www.intuitiveparenting.com/4-reasons-why-mothers-intuition-is-important-in-everyday-parenting/.

79. Atkins, Andrea. "Tune In to Your Mom Intuition." RedBookMag.com, December 29, 2008. http://www.redbookmag.com/life/mom-kids/advice/a4490/mothers-intuition/.

80. "I Think Maybe We Are Here." *Experience Project*. http://www.experienceproject.com/stories/Think-Maybe-We-Are-Here/7056771.

81. Kamrath, Sarah. "Learning to Trust Our Intuition." HealthyHappyChild.com, courtesy of *Natural Child Magazine*, July–August 2011. http://www.happyhealthychild.com/wp-content/uploads/2012/08/Intuition_NaturalChildJuly-Aug11.pdf.

Appendix

Mindful Mothering Tips

In the midst of your busy life, I offer you the following mindful tips to help you remember the importance of keeping a courageous heart.

Self-Reflection

- ℘ Motherhood is a journey to be lived one day at a time; I invite you to savor each day and be open to the valuable lessons it has to offer you.
- ℘ The value of a reflective life is that you're able to make conscious choices and decisions based on past experiences. Self-reflection provides opportunities to determine what is or isn't working in a situation and figure out how to improve upon it.

- ❧ Every day, you have a choice as to how you're going to show up in the world. When you pay attention and reflect upon what is going on in your life and home, you're more apt to catch a problem before it leads to a crisis.

- ❧ When you pay attention—really pay attention—you're able to consciously choose the thoughts and behavior that best serve you and your child.

Seeing Clearly: Take the Opportunity to Open Your Eyes

- ❧ Imagine how your day, your life, might be different if you were able to see yourself through soft, gentle eyes, accepting yourself as is.

- ❧ When you're critical of yourself, it's very easy to be critical of others, especially your children. Self-love begins by recognizing your goodness—honoring yourself for who you are in this moment.

- ❧ Seeing clearly with soft eyes allows you to drop unconscious assumptions and judgments, to delve beneath your perceptions and attachments and open yourself to the truth of who your children are, not who you think they should be.

- ❧ Your hopes and dreams for your child may be beneficial—but only when they're rooted in reality. By letting go of perfection, which often stems from unrealistically high expectations of yourself and others, you allow room for the truth of what is.

Mothering Your Child

- ❧ One of the best ways to acknowledge your child is to first acknowledge their feelings. Your children have a voice. It's important to allow them to use it. When you're able to honor who they are (not who you want them to be), you allow them to grow into who they were meant to be.

☙ Your perception of yourself and your children ought not to be constant but flexible. Flexibility allows you to let go of your firmly held perceptions.

☙ Repetitive patterns and learned behavior begin to develop between every child and parent, and they become rigid if the parent's lens is rigid as well.

☙ Positive messages empower your children and boost their self-worth. Like wildflower seeds planted in a meadow, they blossom and spread over time. Sometime, it's the smallest of seeds or messages that garner the most vibrant flower. Your messages have the power to nurture your child's heart and cultivate their growth.

Making the Connection

☙ Your child is a unique individual. Your ability to see them as such will help strengthen your connection. Your child is also much more apt to feel connected with you when they feel accepted by you—no matter how they're acting.

☙ Children who do not feel connected to their parents become more resistant to parental guidance and rules. The key in-gredient for imparting your parental wisdom and improving your child's behavior is having a healthy connection with them. When your child feels connected with you, they are more open to learn from you. When your relationship with your child improves, so does their behavior.

☙ Connection does not preclude limit-setting or boundaries. Actually, it often requires it!

☙ Love is the first step in developing a connection with your child, but it isn't enough. It also requires time spent, intentionally created just for you and your child—time that is honored and revered.

- Your influence as a parent is either enhanced or diminished by the strength of your connection with your child. This connection is not solely about the time you spend with your child; it's also about attunement—your ability to be receptive and aware of your child and their needs.
- Building and nurturing the bond with your child does not happen once and then you're done—it's a lifelong process.

Children Are Our Teachers

- Children are able to teach us many lessons if we let them. Simply by learning to see your daily interactions with your children from their perspective, you'll learn to shift your own.
- Your children are not only growing, but also providing you with opportunities to grow as well.
- Children are mini-mirrors that reflect our negative and positive qualities.
- Children may also force us to question our own reality, to look at life from a different lens.

Behavior—Yours and Your Child's

- The most effective way you can help your child calm down is first to calm yourself down. When you allow your parental anxiety to guide your parenting decisions, you're quick to jump in and fix just about any perceived "problem" with or for your child. You do this to calm your own anxiety.
- You're not responsible for your child's behavior; you're only responsible for your own.
- Children challenge you to grow, to become the adult, the mom, they want and need you to be: one who's able to stop,

self-reflect, and take responsibility for herself, rather than one who needs her child to behave in order to feel good about herself.

☺ Children are emotional little beings and express their feelings quite naturally—unless we teach them not to. One of the most important lessons you can teach your child is how to *be* with their emotions.

The Art of Discipline

☺ Remember, your child's behavior occurs for a reason—it's not random. Begin to look beyond your child's behavior rather than focusing on behavioral strategies to fix it.

☺ Focusing on and trying to control your child's behavior will not help them learn. As long as you continue to focus on your child's "mis"behavior and employ disciplinary tactics to stop the behavior, you contribute to the problem.

☺ Consequences are important and necessary. Life is full of consequences. Your child will learn far more from natural consequences than they will from your lecture or punishment. However, an unrelated consequence you create is not natural and typically does not teach your child.

☺ Discipline takes practice. It's best to practice it when you and your child are calm, not in the heat of the moment. Remind yourself to take some time off and calm yourself down before you give a consequence.

Truth-Telling

☺ Children learn to lie as a part of their developmental process, but they also learn by watching the examples of others—particularly their parents. Keep in mind: you teach your child to lie when you lie. When you stretch the truth or tell a little white lie, you teach them to lie. Your child also needs to be able to trust that you're telling the truth. Kids need to feel safe with their parents and trust that they're speaking the truth.

⊛ You have an opportunity to create a safe environment for your children in which they can learn to tell the truth, an environment that encourages them to admit their mistakes and learn from them. You ultimately have the opportunity to create a family culture of *truth-telling*.

⊛ Children always fare better when they know the truth. They don't need to know every detail, but trust that if you don't offer some truth, there is a good chance they'll create a truth far worse than the actual truth. Family secrets damage relationships. While family secrets might initially unite families, they have the power to destroy.

⊛ It takes courage to speak the truth. It also takes great courage to speak your own *real truth*—first to yourself and then to others. Hiding from the truth may be easier in the short term. However, your willingness and courage to be open to the truth may grant you a lifetime of freedom—freedom to speak your truth and show up fully, as you are.

Parenting as a Whole

⊛ Your ability to parent in the present is difficult if you keep re-experiencing emotions from your past. When you react from an emotional place, you parent ineffectively.

⊛ Your courage and willingness to be vulnerable and to delve deeper into your places of "unfinished business" will help you heal—and offer you the opportunity to reconnect with your authentic self.

⊛ Parenting as a whole means parenting from your wholeness: first, by being the parent for yourself that you did not have.

Once you're able to nurture yourself, you're then able to wholeheartedly nurture your child.

ꙮ The best gift you can offer your child is to do your own inner work, to heal within so that you can become whole once again. This is how you came into this world, and it is your birthright. The gift of wholeness is priceless, for you and your family.

The Art of Loving Yourself

ꙮ Self-care is not only important but also crucial to your well-being and that of your child, simply because you cannot give what *you* yourself do not have.

ꙮ No one can recognize your need for self-care but you. So if you're waiting for someone to offer you free time each day for self-care, it's not going to happen. No one is going to help you create time for self-care until you recognize the importance of it and make it a priority—for you.

ꙮ Your needs can coexist with the needs of your spouse and kids. Balance is created by intentional planning and taking everyone's needs into consideration. When you are balanced, there is a much better chance your children will be too.

ꙮ A mom's excessive worrying about not being a good-enough mother may override her capacity to see what she's doing exceptionally well. Ruminating on everything you think you've done wrong will only erode your joy and self-confidence.

Trust Your Heart; Trust Yourself

ꙮ It's important to educate yourself as a mom, to utilize the resources available to you to determine various options for you and your children. But after you ascertain information and resources, tap into your own intuitive wisdom. See what feels right for you. As you learn to trust yourself, you'll no longer seek validation from others. The opinions of others will matter less to you than your own.

- The best way to learn to tap into your intuition is to pay attention. Take some time each day to be quiet. When you're able to let go of life's distractions, sensory overload, and the chatter in your brain, your inner wisdom awaits.

- Learn to trust your intuitive heart. Your brain often lives in fear. Your intuitive guidance will not be fear-based. If you find yourself acting out of fear, most likely your brain kicked into gear, creating your fearful thoughts.

- Mothers who learn to rely on their intuition often feel more relaxed. Because they trust their inner knowing, they feel empowered and confident. Although a mother's intuition does not provide her a crystal ball or a guaranteed outcome, it does enable her to say *I made the best decision based on what I felt was right at the time.*

In Gratitude

Mom and Dad, I'm grateful for your love and support. Because of you, I am who I am and do the work that I do. I now know and understand you did the best you could. After all, none of us are given lessons in parenting. We learn from our own parents and their parents. Until we meet on the other side, please know I love you.

Words alone cannot begin to express my love and gratitude to Pattie Welek-Hall, my soul sister, earth angel, and friend. Pattie, as I witnessed your journey while you wrote your memoir, *A Mother's Dance*, you gave me the courage to write. Through the ups and downs and uncertainties, you were right there by my side, quietly saying, "You've got this—keep going." Our paths have crossed before and will cross again; of that I'm sure. Thank you, dear friend.

To my editors—thank you for teaching and supporting me throughout this process. This book needed to be written, and it was clear I was the one to write it. Cindy Barrilleux, you taught me not only the importance of good writing but also many life lessons, and for that I'm grateful. Ellie Maas Davis, where do I begin? From our first week together when I was afraid to write again, you said, "Keep writing, m'lady." I loved working with you, and as we neared the final edits, you gave me the ultimate gift: you shared with me how this book inspired you as a mom. You were the first mom to read my book, and I thank you. Lindsay Sandberg, you have been such a gift and breath of fresh air. Your input was valuable and your editing process seamless. I'd been told that Familius's editors were very kind—and you are. I'm grateful not only for your kindness but also for your guidance and expertise.

Ben Bernstein, without your encouragement, guidance, and gracious introduction to Familius, I'm not sure this book would have reached as many moms in the world. Thank you, friend and colleague. I'm forever inspired by your kindness.

Thank you Yvonne Hunt for believing in my work and helping me share it with the world—and never forget, you are an amazing mom!

To Susan Schwartzman, my amazing publicist—I thank you for your support and belief in my book. Because of your passion and dedication, I know this book will touch the lives of many mothers.

To all my girlfriends and soul sisters, you've stood by my side, believed in my work, and encouraged me to keep going. You've inspired me to be the best I can be—and I thank you. Although my book has taken some of my time from each of you, I've not forgotten about you or how important you are in my life. I'm looking forward to spending more time together and creating sweet girlfriend memories!

To the Familius family, it has been a pleasure working with you. Thank you for believing in my book and message to moms. I look forward to our creative partnership as this book takes on a life of its own. I can't wait to see what's ahead!

To my family—I'm grateful for your never-ending support, love, and encouragement that truly helped me keep going as I wrote the book. Thank you for believing in the importance of our family and for your acknowledgment of my efforts to help other families.

To Greg, for your love, support, and amazing continued effort to cheer me on from the sideline. Thank you for believing in the importance of my work. I love you forever.

And to all the brave mamas in the world. Your strength, love, and fierce commitment to motherhood is a beautiful gift—to your children and the world. Thank you for sharing your journey with me over the years. I am truly inspired by your stories. Savor your courageous journey of motherhood, and never forget how important you are.

About the Author

BONNIE COMPTON, APRN, BC, CPNP, has worked with families for more than thirty years as a child and adolescent therapist, parent coach, and pediatric nurse practitioner. She is passionate about making a difference in the lives of children and families. By giving parents the tools to parent mindfully, Bonnie inspires them to wake up to what to really matters. Whether it is through individual therapy, coaching, or parenting classes she offers, Bonnie believes that it is possible to make positive changes in any family situation—and it's never too late! She is a writer, speaker, workshop, and retreat facilitator and hosts her own podcast radio program, *Wholehearted Parenting Radio*, which is available on iTunes, Web Talk Radio, Radioactive Broadcasting Network, and Stitcher Radio. Bonnie has appeared as a parenting expert on numerous television and radio shows, and has written parenting articles in magazines and newspapers. She is also a certified ScreamFree Parent Leader.

Bonnie lives in Charleston, SC, with her husband. She is a mom of four adult children and believes that being a mother has been her most important job. She also loves being Gramma to her three beautiful granddaughters.

About Familius

Visit Our Website: www.familius.com

Join Our Family: There are lots of ways to connect with us! Subscribe to our newsletters at www.familius.com to receive uplifting daily inspiration, essays from our Pater Familius, a free ebook every month, and the first word on special discounts and Familius news.

Get Bulk Discounts: If you feel a few friends and family might benefit from what you've read, let us know and we'll be happy to provide you with quantity discounts. Simply email us at orders@familius.com.

Connect:
www.facebook.com/paterfamilius
@familiustalk, @paterfamilius1
www.pinterest.com/familius

FAMILIUS

The most important work
you ever do will be within the
walls of your own home.

CPSIA information can be obtained
at www.ICGtesting.com
Printed in the USA
FSOW01n1848200817
37760FS